Three Hundred Tang Poems

Three Hundred Tang Poems

Translated by
GEOFFREY R. WATERS,
MICHAEL FARMAN & DAVID LUNDE

Introduction by
JEROME P. SEATON

White Pine Press / Buffalo, New York

White Pine Press
P.O. Box 236
Buffalo, New York 14201

State of the Arts

NYSCA

Publication of this book was made possible, in part, by a grant from the National Endowment of the Arts, which believes that a great nation deserves great art, and with public funds from the New York State Council on the Arts, a State Agency.

NATIONAL ENDOWMENT FOR THE ARTS
A great nation deserves great art.

ACKNOWLEDGMENTS

Grateful acknowledgement to the journals in which these poems have appeared or will appear:

David Lunde's translations first appeared in the following journals, to whose editors he would like to express his gratitude:

Blue Unicorn: "Regarding This Spring (Spring Outlook)," "At Deer Park Hermitage"
Burning Cloud Review: "The Summer Palace"
Calapooya Collage: "Thinking of My Brothers on a Moonlit Night (Somewhere My Brothers May See this Moon)," "Sad Thoughts in Spring (Thinking of Her Husband in Spring)," "Spring Morning (Spring Sunrise)"
Chaminade Literary Review: "Moonlit Night," "To a Buddhist Monk Returning to Japan," "Drinking Alone Beneath the Moon," "Untitled [Li Shangyin]"
Chelsea: "Written While Traveling at Night," "On Yueyang Tower"
Crab Creek Review: "Moored on the Qin Huai River,"
Cumberland Poetry Review: "Ballad of the Border"
Grasslimb: "Listening to a Monk of Shu Play His Lute"
Jeopardy: "Moored at Night by Maple Bridge"
Literary Imagination: "Missing Li Bai at the End of the Earth," "Climbing High (From a Height)"
Many Mountains Moving: "Meeting Li Guinian in the South," "Climbing the Tower"
Northwest Review: "Ballad of the Army Carts"
Oasis: "Elegies on Ancient Sites (3)," "Song of the Border"
Plainsongs: "Jade Stairs Grievance (Resentment on the Jade Stairs)"
Potomac Review: "Passing the Night on Jiande River"
Renditions: "A Song of Painting," "Searching for Dao Master Chang at South Stream"
Salamander: "The Pitiful Young Prince"

Acknowledgments continue on page 271.

First Edition.
ISBN: 978-1-935210-26-9

Library of Congress Control Number: 2011931993

Contents

Five-Word Old Style Poems

Zhang Jiuling

Li Bai

Du Fu

Wang Wei

Meng Haoran

Five-Word Old Style Yuefu

Seven-Word Old Style Poems

Seven-Word Old Style Yuefu

Five-Word Regulated Verse

Wang Wei

Meng Haoran

Seven-Word Quatrain Yuefu

Editor's Note

Geoff Waters unexpectedly passed away while a previous book of his translations, *White Crane: Love Songs of the Sixth Dalai Lama,* published by White Pine Press in 2007, was at the printer. I had spoken several times with Geoff about publishing his translation of the Chinese anthology *300 Tang Poems* when he completed it. That unfortunately was not to be. In the wake of his death I approached several mutual friends and translators from the Chinese to see if there was interest among them in finishing up the work Geoffrey had done over so many years. They not only were interested but Jerome "Sandy" Seaton, Michael Farman, and David Lunde agreed to work with me to complete this important book. Jerome Seaton contributed an introduction and his critical eye to the translations; and Michael Farman and David Lunde worked to complete the unfinished poems in the manuscript. We all owe a great debt to them for making this volume possible. Geoffrey left some notes for a preface and acknowledgments to the eventual publication of the book, and I have included them below as they give both some insight into his interest and an acknowledgment to his teachers and friends along the way.

Dennis Maloney
Editor/Publisher
White Pine Press

Preface

I began studying Chinese as a college student in the late 1960s. The first book of Chinese poetry I bought was a bilingual Taiwan reprint of *Jade Mountain*, Witter Bynner's 1929 translation of the standard eighteenth-century Chinese anthology *Three Hundred Tang Poems*. It was my first encounter with the Tang poets. As my Chinese improved, my first translations were "corrections" of Bynner's sometimes quaint English, written in the margin. I still have the book, but the bulk of my handwritten efforts have not stood the test of time and taste.

Appetite whetted by *Jade Mountain*, I sought other translations from the Chinese, and soon discovered Arthur Waley. Waley's story seemed too good to be true: a young man in his twenties, self-taught in Chinese and within a few years publishing marvelous, expert translations to critical acclaim. By the time *Jade Mountain* was published in 1929, Waley's influential *A Hundred and Seventy Chinese Poems* had been in print for more than ten years, translations respected as English poetry themselves, not just as one medium by which Chinese poetry entered the mainstream of British and American literary culture.

As I read more widely, I found other voices that had made Chinese poetry into memorable English, among them Ezra Pound's *Cathay* (1915), sometimes more a variation on the originals than a translation, but often dazzling nonetheless, and A. C. Graham's wonderful *Poems of the Late T'ang*. Even so, for me Waley was always the gold standard.

Encountering his work only a few years after his death in 1966, I daydreamed of becoming his artistic successor. That was the over-romanticized musing of a young man barely twenty, whose own poetic output was modest in both quality and quantity, and whose lifetime of Chinese study was still ahead of him. But now, almost forty years later, looking back at those days, I know that reading Waley's *A Hundred and Seventy Chinese Poems*, more than any of the others, helped me decide to translate Tang poetry.

Jade Mountain was also important as an example of another kind: Bynner, like too many published translators of Chinese poetry before and later, did not know Chinese. He worked from draft notes provided by his collaborator, Dr. Kiang Kang-hu. I now see many poems where either Dr. Kiang misread the original, or Bynner misunderstood Dr. Kiang's notes, or Bynner's poetic license simply took him in the wrong direction. As a specialist in these texts, I have mistrusted that kind of collaborative literary translation ever since, despite its occasional successes.

Waley had not touched the majority of the *Three Hundred Tang Poems*, so I decided to make a new translation. I nibbled at it during my tour of duty as an artillery officer and then during my PhD studies in Classical Chinese. Afterwards, it languished as I focused on the life of my family, my banking career, and other part-time scholarly and writing projects like the *Nine Elegies*, Tibetan poetry, Old Chinese phonology and Manchu grammar. But it was always in the back of my mind, waiting for the time to be right.

Eleven years living and working in Hong Kong along the way gave me the opportunity to learn Cantonese in addition to my Mandarin. Cantonese is valuable for the study of Tang Poetry because it preserves a tonal system and pronunciation much like Middle Chinese, the language of the Tang poets. Also, living in Hong Kong, and frequent travel in China, gave me the chance to acquire some indispensable reference books and quite a few anthologies of Tang poetry that were not as easily available elsewhere.

Armed with these resources, I decided several years ago to return to the *Three Hundred Tang Poems*. After finishing about a third of the longer poems, I started translating the quatrains, or four-line poems, that make up the last few sections of the collection. I thought their smaller scale (only twenty or twenty-eight characters each) would fit my fragmented work schedule better.

I hope you find something beautiful in the words of these dead poets of the Tang. I never tire of them.

Geoff Waters
Glendale, California
September 2006

Acknowledgments

First, I must thank my many Chinese teachers: especially Friedrich Bischoff, Irving Yucheng Lo, and the late Wu-chi Liu. Professor Bischoff, among many things, taught me never to underestimate the text, no matter how simple it looks. In Professor Lo's courses on Tang Poetry I was exposed to a wide spectrum of writers and styles. I learned from Professor Liu's encyclopedic knowledge of Chinese literature and history that Chinese poetry reads best when placed by careful scholarship squarely in the context of the life and times of the poets.

Second, I must express my gratitude to those poets and translators who have encouraged me by their kind words and helpful comments in reading drafts of this book over the past few years. First among them is Willis Barnstone. I did my first serious literary translations in his graduate seminar on poetry translation at Indiana University over thirty years ago: the complete poems of Yu Xuanji. Willis and his daughter, the poet Aliki Barnstone, included twenty or so of them in their anthology *A Book of Women Poets from Antiquity to Now* (Shocken Books 1980, and reprints). Without the help of Aliki and Willis Barnstone, both then and now, this book would not be in your hands. I am also grateful to my fellow translators Gary Snyder, Sam Hamill, Sandy Seaton, Steve Bradbury, Tony Barnstone, Lucas Klein, John Balcom, David Hinton, Mike Farman, Charles Hartman, and especially David Hawkes for advice and encouragement.

Finally, let me thank my wife, Joyce Rehfuss, and my sons Asa Ferry and Matt Waters, for their usually patient indulgence of the hours I spent immersed in Tang China on so many weekend mornings over the years.

Geoff Waters

Introduction

The *Three Hundred Tang Poems* may very well have been the best selling, the most avidly read, and the most diligently studied, of any poetry book in history anywhere in the world, from the moment in 1763 or 1764 when it first appeared in bookshops throughout China, until well after the start of the twentieth century. It remains a widely popular book among the general readership in China: as I write in 2009, it gets roughly 120,000 Google hits in a Chinese language search. Educated readers of Chinese all over the world continue to enjoy its very broad and representative selection of poets, including great names like Li Bai (Li Po), Du Fu (Tu Fu), and Wang Wei, as well as its splendid sampling of poems by the rest of the poets who helped to make the Tang the "Golden Age" of Chinese poetry.

The beginning of "modern literature" in China was dramatically marked by the May Fourth Movement of 1917. One revolutionary goal of the Movement was to make spoken colloquial "Mandarin" the language of both poetry and prose, and this revolution was indeed successful. Yet even until the early twentieth century *all* poetry and the most prestigious forms of prose were created in wen yen, the language we call *classical* or *literary* Chinese. Wen yen made conscious use of the peculiarities of the Chinese writing system, what we know as *Chinese characters*, to allow the polysyllabic spoken language to be condensed into an extremely concise, almost monosyllabic form, while also enhancing visual and allusive possibilities for the author. This telegraphic classical literary language allowed poets to be at the same time both visually descriptive and almost subliminally suggestive, both powerfully imagistic and delicately evocative. No Chinese poet still writes in classical Chinese (though its influence remains evident in scholarly writing and even in newspaper prose), but anthologies of classical poetry, including *Three Hundred Tang Poems*, unquestionably remain extremely influential in the formation of the sense of the potential for beauty in language for the modern writer. The artistic manipulation of the written language that made the Tang Dynasty China's literary Golden Age remains one of the great influences on China's literary present.

The instant success of *Three Hundred Tang Poems* isn't surprising, since its contents were, after all, the essence refined from the best of many earlier collections and anthologies, the finest poems from the greatest poets. If you're an avid reader of Chinese poetry you will be delighted to find old favorites here. All the forms of poetry as it was practiced in the Tang were represented, as well as its best and its most famous poets, a fact that certainly contributed to its success among readers who were aspiring writers.

The anthologist responsible for this best of the best of anthologies was a man named Sun Zhu (1711–1778). Like most traditionally educated authors who wrote for money in eighteenth century China, Sun Zhu preferred to remain as anonymous as possible, since a Chinese "gentleman," like a European aristocrat, was not supposed to do anything for money. The proposed aim of the anthology was didactic: to teach conventional Neo-Confucian morality and *Wen*, the cultural values that arose from the appreciation and the creation of literature, and which, in turn, created the Confucian gentleman, or *jun zi*. Such issues aside, poetry writing, or at least verse writing, and general knowledge regarding poetry (for example the ability to identify a quotation, or even to continue a line or a whole poem when offered a part of a line), was probably as important in the social mobility of a young Chinese gentleman as jumping a fence on horseback, or knowing the difference between the bows and scrapes one owed a Count and a Duke was for an aspiring member of the eighteenth- or nineteenth-century English gentry.

Sun Zhu was an excellent judge, even a connoisseur, of Tang poetry, and extremely knowledgeable with regard to literary criticism, and any student who went to his book for guidance on these matters would be very well served. In fact, the book has also become one of the key twentieth century primers for Western readers of Chinese poetry. After the pioneering translations of Li Bai by Ezra Pound, and contemporaneously with the early translations of Arthur Waley, *The Jade Mountain, A Chinese anthology*, a good but now very dated version by the poet Witter Bynner and his Chinese informant Kiang Kang-hu, published in 1929, was the main source of Tang poetry in English for more than twenty years. This new translation of Sun Zhu's selection by Geoff Waters, "with a little help from his friends," may very well touch a chord, ring like a wonderful *déjà vu*: Geoff's bright new American English, and his rare combination of knowledge of classical Chinese with a poet's voice, allow contemporary readers to hear the true greatness of this group of poems which have provided American readers, and American poets and translators, inspiration for nearly a century. Here those already familiar with Tang poetry as it was revoiced in twentieth century English will find Li Bai's signature piece, "Drinking Alone Beneath the Moon," the quatrain "Leaving Early from White Emperor City," Pound's favorite "Song of Changgan," and an excellent version of the quatrain "Jade Stairs Grievance," another poem that enthralled, and confounded, the great Pound. Among the selection of Du Fu's are some of his best known in both China and the world, including the great love poem for his wife, "Moonlit Night," the searing social commentary poem "Ballad of the Army Carts" and several other great poems often attempted by American translators, I assume basing their readings on Bynner, including "Welcoming a Guest," "Passing the Night at the General's Headquarters," and "Ballad: On Watching a Student of Miss Gong Sun the First Perform the Sword Dance." Among the poems by Wang Wei included that will surely stir memories, or pure enjoyment for first time readers, are "Reply to Vice-Prefect Zhang," "South Mountain Retreat," and the striking quatrains "Farewell in the Mountains," "Bamboo Refuge," and "At Deer Park Hermitage." The latter is a multifaceted jewel, twenty syllables that have, in the eighty years since their introduction to the world's English-speaking public, inspired, at last count, more than twenty well known poets and scholars, including among the more recently celebrated, Kenneth Rexroth, Burton Watson, Sam Hamill, the Barnstones, father and son, and Gary Snyder, to attempt an American language version.

The book offers its reader the best, or at least the most remarkable, of the work of other lesser known poets as well. From Bai Juyi, a "poets' poet" almost at the level of the big three of Tang, we get the very lengthy "Song of Endless Sorrow," and a maybe more representative piece "Grass on the Old Plain." Longer poems by Cen Shen, Han Yu, and a poem *about* Han Yu by Li Shangyin show another side of the usually short if not always sweet Tang poetic sensitivity. The martial pride as well as the more pacifistic social concern of the period is found in many of these longer poems. I can't not mention Jia Dao's "Seeking a Hermit but Not Finding Him, Liu Zongyuan's "River Snow," Meng Haoran's "Spring Morning," or the unknown poet Li Pin's "Crossing the Han River." Among my favorites are Lu Lun's border poems and the quatrains by Du Fu's cousin Du Mu that so brilliantly express the remorse of a middle-aged man who finds he has squandered a career and the faith of a loving family for a life as a privileged wastrel. This is a great collection in the original, and as you will see, its translators have lived up to the challenge of making it a fine one in American English too.

Since the original anthology's intended purpose was didactic, it is not surprising that the selection of poems was skewed toward those that could be construed to support the authoritarian reading of Zhu Xi's Neo-Confucianism, an ideology favored by the Manchu conquerors of China who ruled as the Qing Dynasty. But Sun Zhu, the anthologist, was an interesting man with a multifaceted personality. True, there is no poetry by wildman monks like Han Shan in his book, and not a single poem by any of the venerable monk poets Jiaoran, Lingyi, Guanxiu, or even Wuben, (though a sample of his lay poetry, under his lay name, Jia Dao, is included) though these monks were counted among the friends of the great lay poets who are in the book. On the other hand, Wang Wei, the most Buddhist of the poets who are included, is given more space, in spite of the very low number of his poems extant in the Qing, compared to those of either Li Bai or Du Fu. Sun Zhu, staying true to the dictates of the radically independent critical school to which he belonged, even included love poetry by the likes of Li Shangyin, poetry that was suppressed as salacious in earlier more rigorously Neo-Confucian anthologies of the Qing.

While Tang was a high point of power for women, at least upper-class women, in traditional Chinese history, Qing hinged its authoritarian government on suppression of all Chinese, and tried to use Neo-Confucian prudery as a wedge to make women scapegoats. So even though Sun Zhu's wife helped with the creation of the anthology itself, and even though Yuan Mei, one of the strongest advocates of the critical school that helped form Sun's views, was also an insurgent in the fight against the Manchu's attitude toward women, it is perhaps not too surprising that there is only one poem by a woman poet included. But whatever ideological positions the book might have been compiled to support, it is first and foremost a selection of great poetry, much of which rises above all such considerations, even as the anthology as a whole exhibits them, and Mr. and Ms. Sun, working together, deserve applause for that.

Certainly the anthology was intended as a textbook. It's also true that most poets of the time larded their poems with quotes from one or the other set of models, Tang or Song. On the one hand it is clear that much or even most of *Qing* poetry was terribly derivative; on the other hand, as you read these poems in translation you'll see that exposure to such models couldn't do anybody harm. And the presence of such a wildly successful good model had an exceptionally positive effect outside the ranks of school boys, among the population at large. Among the dozens and dozens of diverse characters in the great Chinese novel *The Scholars* (*Rulin Waishi*), perhaps the most fascinating of them all to us denizens of the poetry-blind twenty first century are the ordinary shop keepers and craftsmen who meet regularly to read, write and discuss poetry. Readers raised on the poetry in this anthology were intellectual and aesthetic sophisticates, whatever else they were.

The young Chinese folks, and their elders, who came to this book for the reasons described above, were not surprised to find the book divided not by theme or by poet, but by "forms." I think we'd be surprised to come to a book like *The Oxford Book of English Verse* and to find it organized not in chronological order, or arranged in alphabetical order by authors, but rather by sonnets, heroic couplets, blank verse, and, say, to lighten this up a little, limericks or triolets. But this is the traditional way of arranging Chinese anthologies.

Before I go on to give those forms a little further examination, let me point out and explain something that you may already have noticed: we're offering you 320 poems for the price of the advertised 300. The three hundred of the title was intended by Sun Zhu to suggest the number supposed to have been chosen by Confucius himself to make up the *Shi Jing*, the *Poetry Classic*. The number of poems in the *Shi Jing* is *actually* 305 poems, but the work is almost always, for the sake of elegance or abbreviation, referred to as "the three hundred poems," so we may excuse *our* anthologist if he follows the historical locution. In fact any connection with Confucius was a very good *marketing decision*, for Sun Zhu, and for any other Chinese who wanted to sell a book, an idea, or even himself, for more than the last two thousand years.

But to get back to forms: For Sun Zhu's younger readers at least, the mastery of form was, as I mentioned above, at least as important as the imbibing of moral, ethical, political, aesthetic and even spiritual values from the book. For us there's no real reason outside an honorable curiosity to know anything about the forms of classical Chinese poetry, so perhaps we can let it suffice to say that whatever it looks like in the table of contents, there are essentially only two forms included. The first of the two kinds, *gu shi*, meaning literally "old style," refers to poems written in a form that was developed in the Han Dynasty, about 500 years before the beginning of the Tang. *Lu shi*, meaning "regulated verse," is a brief way of referring to a new form deriving from "old style" which was still in development when the Tang began in 618.

The "old style" poem rhymes on every other even-numbered line, and any given poem may either have only lines of five or seven characters, but the poem may be of any length. The "regulated verse," *strictly speaking*, is a poem limited to eight lines, and follows the *gu shi* in having lines of either five or seven characters. Like the *gu shi*, it also has a regular rhyme scheme, rhyming on the even-numbered lines (the first line may sometimes be rhymed as well). However, two very different features of the *lu shi* are what define it as *lu*, or "regulated." First, each of the characters in each line must follow a certain set "tonal pattern," a truly complex feat that can't be reflected in translation, since English is not a tonal language. Du Fu, advocate and practitioner of self-discipline in all its best forms, was among the greatest at the effective use of this sort of patterning, while Li Bai, who, thank you Scarlett, really didn't give a damn, did just enough of it to prove he could.

The second feature of the *lu shi* is the creation of grammatical parallelism in the middle two couplets of the verse. This feature of regulation *can be* reflected in English, and it is in quite a few poems in this anthology. In the originals it is sometimes used to create deep and subtle gradation of meaning and feeling, but it is also very often, even in a fine poem, just a technical flourish, a decoration for decoration's sake, and in these cases the translator may justifiably choose to ignore it, if rigid formal reflection does harm to the bringing over of *meaning*. You can trust these particular translators to have spent a great deal of time and thought before abjuring the need for parallelism in some of their English versions.

The category of "form" that includes some of the best known and most admired poems of the Tang Dynasty, both in China and in the West, is the quatrain, or *jue ju*. This is essentially a *lu shi* foreshortened to four lines without the requirement for parallelism. It may have five or seven characters per line. This form includes some real gems. Most of the *jue ju* known best in the West are of the five character per line type.

Chinese critics began almost immediately in the Tang to argue about and to categorize *ad nauseam* the nature of the form, and they have posited that there are regulated and unregulated quatrains, and that the regulated can consist of *the first and last couplets of a regulated verse*, of the *second or third couplet plus the final couplet*, or, in rare cases, of *two middle (that is parallel) couplets*. I'm not convinced there's much evidence that any of the great poets followed any of these formal prescriptions with any regularity though, and in fact I believe the operant principle of the *jue ju*, like its well known Japanese counterpart the haiku, lies in its original and imaginative brevity, period.

As you will know by now from the editor's foreword, this anthology was conceived and largely finished by the late scholar-translator Geoff Waters. Translating poems chosen for you by another person, as Geoff did in choosing to do the *300 Poems*, can be a particularly difficult task. You don't always agree with the anthologist's choices, and sometimes it's nearly impossible to convince yourself that a particular poem deserves *your best work*. Geoff didn't adore every poem that Sun Zhu picked, but he felt that it was important to present the cultural mindset, the values, of a traditional scholar from the final period of traditional Chinese history, by presenting his choices in a language that would make those values, through the poems themselves, clear. Geoff died suddenly at the age of fifty-eight, thinking, planning, dreaming about the translations that he would make after he retired from banking, *soon*. We both got our degrees from Indiana University, studying under the brilliant Sinologist and great teacher Friedrich Bischoff, about a decade apart. We talked about Geoff's future by e-mail pretty often, and often spoke of his plans to retire from banking and to get back to full time scholarship and translation. I urged him to retire, but it was a selfish argument on my part. I really wanted someone to work with and to talk to about translating. This anthology was a pet project of Geoff's in his last few years. It wasn't finished, and then he was gone. But several other lovers of Chinese poetry, people he knew mainly through e-mail, with a few face to face meetings of a day or two at conferences of the American Literary Translators Association, appreciated his work, and they, Dennis Maloney, Michael Farman, and David Lunde came together to complete some of Geoff's unfinished translations, to add some of their own, and to edit parts that were obviously in early draft form. Some of Geoff's notes on the poems were so coded to himself as to be undecipherable by others, so those provided have ended up fewer than he intended. I'm glad to have made a small contribution to the editing process, and proud to have been asked to write this introduction. It is a wonderful anthology in the original, and Geoff, with help from Mike, David, and Dennis, has found a new voice for it, an American voice, clear, concise, uncluttered, and strong. This book is a fitting memorial to a multi-talented man: Geoff Waters hereby joins Sun Zhu and the poets he anthologized, to be forever known as a man who discharged his many roles in the world with responsibility and honor, as a family man, as an accomplished man of letters and, therefore, as a true gentleman, a *Jun Zi*. I think he'd be proud to be known for being that.

Jerome P. Seaton

Three Hundred Tang Poems

五言古詩
Five-Word Old-Style Poems

Zhang Jiuling

Afterthoughts (1)

A lone swan rises from the sea;
it dares not look toward its old pond,
but sees instead, a pair of kingfishers
nesting in a protective tree.
High up in those precious branches,
are they free from fear of arrows?
Vivid plumage draws attention,
and with it, perhaps some evil end.
Now I must fly to a distant world,
beyond the reach of hunters' arrows.

MEF

Afterthoughts (2)

Orchid leaves, in spring, are thick and lush;
laurel blooms, in fall, are pure and shining.
At their peak, so vigorous and alive;
each, at the right time, the glory of the season.
Do they sense the hermit, living deep in their woods,
who feels such joy to smell their fragrance in the air?
These plants by nature are perfect in their place;
why flourish to be broken by some lovely hand?

GW

Afterthoughts (3)

I left office and retired alone to this dim forest,
my mind washed clean of cares by pure solitude.
I want to share my thoughts with that high-flying bird,
so it can carry them to someone far away.
Day and night, such futile moods,
who among my peers does my sincerity move?
So distant now from those who fly or fail,
who will console me for my barren loyalty?

G W

Afterthoughts (4)

In the south, a tangerine tree grows;
its leaves stay green all winter long.
Is this because the weather there is mild,
or does it have a heart familiar with the touch of cold?
It would make a fine gift for an honored guest;
why, then, do you leave it there, so far away?
To each of us, a destiny that holds us firm;
the circle's closed; there's no way to break free.
Peaches and plums are the popular choice,
but doesn't this tree also make fine shade?

G W

Li Bai

Coming Down from Southmost Mountain, Stopping for Wine at Husi's Mountain Hermitage

At nightfall, coming down from the green mountainside,
the mountain moon was following me home.
I looked back along the path, where I had come,
down a narrow valley dark with trees.
It was there I met you and you led me to your house.
Your boy came out and opened the gate for us;
through green bamboos, down a dark path,
we walked, creepers catching on our clothes.
As we talked happily, I found the peace I sought,
for a while, pouring for each other your fine wine.
We sang so long the song of "Pines in the Wind,"
that when we finished, few stars remained in the dark sky.
I got drunk that night, and you were happy, too;
for a while, we forgot the world and all its cares.

GW

Drinking Alone Beneath the Moon

One jar of wine among the flowers,
no dear friend to drink with:
I offer a cup to the moon.
With my shadow there are three of us,
but the moon doesn't know how to drink,
and my shadow can't help but follow me.
Still, I'll make do with their company,
have fun and make the most of spring.
I sing and the moon rolls around,
I dance and my shadow leaps about.
While I'm lively we enjoy each other,
when I get too drunk we go our own ways.
Let's keep this undemanding friendship
till we join together in far Cloud-river.

DL

Sad Thoughts in Spring

In Yan, the grass is but green threads;
in Qin, the mulberry trees are thick with leaves.
By the time you turn your heart toward home,
my own will have already broken.
The spring wind and I no longer know each other:
why should it part my silk gauze curtain?

DL

Du Fu

Gazing at Mount Tai

How to describe Mount Tai?
Its green towers above all of Chi and Lu!
Here Nature concentrated divine beauty;
its north and south sides split dark from dawn.
Chest pounding, you reach the birthplace of clouds;
bursting eyes fill with birds returning to nest.
Someday I must climb to the very top,
look down on all the little mountains at once.

DL

Poem for Wei Ba

Often a man's life is such
that he seldom sees his friends,
like the constellations Shen and Shang
which never share the same sky.
If not this evening, then what evening
should we share this lamp light?
How long can our youth and vigor last?
The hair at our temples is already gray.
We inquire about old acquaintances
to find that half are ghosts—
shocked cries betray
the torment of our hearts.
How could I have known
that it would be twenty years
before I again entered
your honored home.
When we parted last
you were yet unmarried;
now your sons and daughters

line up in a smiling row
to greet their father's friend.
They ask where I have come from
but before I can answer all questions
you chase them off
to bring wine and cups.
In the night rain, chives are cut
for the freshly steamed rice
mixed with yellow millet.
Saying how difficult it has been
for us to meet at last,
you pour ten cups in a row!
But even after ten cups
I'm not drunk, being so moved
by your lasting friendship.
Tomorrow we will be separated
by the peaks of mountains,
each of our worldly affairs
lost to the other's sight.

DL

A Woman of Quality

Matchless in breeding and beauty,
a fine lady has taken refuge in this forsaken valley.
She is of good family, she says, but her fortune has withered away;
now she lives as the grass and trees.
When the heartlands fell to the rebels, her brothers were put to death;
birth and position counted for nothing—
she was not even allowed to bring home their bones for burial.
The world turns quickly against those who have had their day—
fortune is a lamp-flame flickering in the wind.
Her husband is a fickle fellow who has a lovely new wife.
Even the vetch-tree is more constant, folding its leaves each dusk,
and mandarin ducks always sleep beside their mates.
But he has eyes only for his new woman's smile,

and his ears are deaf to his first wife's weeping.
High in the mountains spring water is clear as truth,
but it reaches the lowlands muddied with rumor.
Her serving-maid returns from selling her pearls;
she drags a creeper over to cover holes in the roof.
The flowers the lady picks are not for her hair,
and the handfuls of cypress are a bitter stay against hunger.
Her pretty blue sleeves are too thin for the cold;
as evening falls she leans on the tall bamboo.

DL

Dreaming of Li Bai (1)

Parting with the dead,
one eventually stops sobbing;
when parting with the living
sorrow never ends.
You're exiled to Yelang in Jiangnan,
a place plagued by malaria,
and no news of you, old friend.
But you enter my dream tonight
for you are always in my thoughts.
You've been tangled in the nets of the law;
how did you free your wings to fly here?
It makes me fear this soul of yours
is not of one still living.
The road between us is too long to measure.
When your soul set out this way,
you could see the green maples,
but when your soul returns
it will travel through dark passes.
As I wake, the sinking moon
floods the roof-beams with its light,
and I stare about, half-expecting
it will shine on your face.
Between us the water is deep

and the waves broad and tall—
don't let the water-dragons
seize you, my friend!

DL

Dreaming of Li Bai (2)

All day long clouds float restlessly,
still my wanderer does not arrive.
Three nights in a row I've dreamed of you:
I can see the kindly concern in your mind,
but you always leave in a rush,
saying ruefully, "Coming here wasn't easy—
the wind blows wild waves on river and lake;
I was afraid I'd lose my oars and capsize."
You go out the door scratching your white hair
as if disappointed in your life's dreams.
The capital city is filled with officials—
why should this man be made so wretched?
Who says the Emperor spreads a wide net
in his search for men of talent?
Li is getting old, and still struggling to survive.
Making a name to last a thousand autumns
is a pointless post-mortem affair.

DL

Wang Wei

A Farewell

We dismounted, shared wine.
"Where are you going?" I asked.
"My dreams are shattered," you said,
"I'm retiring to South Mountain—
ask no more," and off you went.
White clouds drift on forever.

DL

To Qiwu Qian , Homeward Bound After Failing the Examinations

If sages ruled, no failed scholars would live in shadow;
ability and intelligence could come and go at the palace.
Men out of office would return, like Xie An of East Mountain,
and no longer starve to death gathering ferns for food.
You came and took the test, and yet the Emperor's gate is still out
of reach.
None can claim it is due to lack of talent.
When you traveled here through Jianghuai, it was Cold Food Day;
now, in both Capitals, people mend their spring clothes.
Seeing you off with a drink, your long road ahead,
my heart will travel with you on your journey.
Now, you will float away in your boat with cassia oars,
and before long you will open your rustic gate.
As I watch you sail away through distant trees,
I will be left alone here in this twilight city.
Although our talents have been overlooked,
we're friends in a world where friends are hard to find.

GW

Green Creek

To reach Chrysanthemum River,
it's said you must follow Green Creek.
Through the mountain's endless twists and turns,
the path is only a hundred *li*.

There's turmoil in water crashing over rocks,
but stillness deep among the pines.
Water plants float, borne by gentle ripples;
young reeds are mirrored where the water's clear.

My mind is already still and calm,
clear and tranquil as the stream.
I think of resting on this boulder,
ready with fishing hook and line.

MEF

Farmers on Wei River

The setting sun lights the village;
to empty lanes, cows and sheep return.
An old man is concerned for a herdboy,
leaning on his staff, waiting by the gate.
Pheasants cluck, the barley is now in flower;
silkworms sleep among the last mulberry leaves.
Farmers shoulder spades and stand
to chat with each other for a while.
Seeing this tranquil life they lead,
I sadly sing the Ode, "It cannot be."

GW

A Song of Xi Shi

The whole world values lovely women;
how could Xi Shi have remained unsung?
One morning, washing silk in a Yue creek;
that same evening, a Wu palace concubine.
While still poor, she was one of many;
once fortune smiled, how precious she became.
She had servants now to powder her face,
and dress her up in fine silk gowns.
The more the King prized her, the more beautiful she seemed;
he was bewitched, lost touch with right and wrong.
Old friends from her days of washing silk,
how could they come to the palace in a carriage?
What point then, for any local girl
to practice Xi Shi's frown and think it beautiful?

G W

Meng Haoran

Autumn: Climbing Orchid Mountain, Sent to Zhang

Here among white clouds on North Mountain,
you've found contentment in seclusion.
Starting the long climb to meet you,
my heart soars with the wild geese to the heights.
I might have given way to sadness as the sun went down
if it weren't for the joy of clear autumn air.

Below me, I see villagers returning home,
waiting on sands by the ferry crossing.
At the far horizon, trees, small as water chestnuts;
by the river bank, a crescent-moon-shaped sandbar.
Perhaps you'll come and meet me, bring some wine;
we'll drink together to the Double Ninth.

MEF

Summertime at South Pavilion; Missing Xin the Elder

West, the sun slips quietly behind the mountain;
east, the moon rises slowly over the lake.

I loose my hair, enjoy the cool of evening,
lie down in peace near the open window.
Breezes waft in lotus fragrance;
dewdrops chime on bamboo leaves.

I'd like to find my lute and play it,
sadly, there's no one here to share the music.
I'm wishing you were here with me, dear friend,
but your presence only haunts my midnight dreams.

MEF

Overnight at Master Ye's Mountain Lodge, Waiting in Vain for My Old Friend Ding

The sun begins to sink below the western peaks;
valleys one by one are steeped in shadow.
The moon rises through the pines, the night grows chill;
breezes coax clear music from the spring.

Woodsmen make ready to return home;
in light mist, birds begin to find a resting-place.
You promised you'd be here with me today;
I'm waiting with my lute, along this vine-draped path.

MEF

Wang Changling

With My Cousin, Enjoying the Moonlight in the Southern Study, Thinking About District Defender Cui at Shanyin

Resting at ease in the Southern Study,
I open the curtain just as the moon appears.
Light through trees casts moving shadows on the water,
reflecting ripples through my window.
Full moon and new, always in their turn,
shine down on past and present.
Tonight, you are somewhere, beside a clear river,
down there in Yue, singing sadly.
A thousand miles apart, what can we do?
A faint breeze brings the scent of orchids.

GW

Qiu Wei

Looking for a Recluse on West Mountain but Not Finding Him at Home

On the highest peak, his grass hut;
I climbed ten miles to visit him.
I knock at his gate, no servant answers;
I peek in, just simple furniture.
Perhaps he went out in his rustic cart,
or off to trail a hook in the autumn river?
We've missed each other, so I won't see him,
but having made the climb, I stay a while.
The grass shines after rain;
pines whisper at evening outside his window.
I feel at one with this secluded place,
my heart washed clean by its sights and sounds.
Although my host was not here to share it,
I realize a great sense of peace has come over me.
Finally, I go back down the mountain;
in the end, no need to wait for his return.

GW

Qiwu Qian

In Spring, Boating on Ruoye Creek

Brooding on thoughts that have no resolution,
I give no thought to where we're drifting.
An evening breeze sends the boat onward,
following the drift of fallen flowers on the creek.
At nightfall, we turn into the western gorge,
as the southern dipper shines between the hills.
Mist spreads above the sandy shore;
the moon sets behind us in the trees.
Thinking of how uncertain our lives have grown,
I wish I were that old man with his fishing pole.

GW

Chang Jian

Spending the Night at Wang Changling's Hermitage

The clear creek seems almost endless,
far-off, above your place, a single cloud.
Now a faint moon appears among the pines,
as if to shed its light on your behalf.
Flowers cast their moving shadows on your little pavilion,
above the moss growing in your courtyard full of herbs.
I, too, would like to say farewell to life's entanglements,
and fly as one with phoenix and crane on West Mountain.

GW

Cen Shen

With Gao Shi and Xue Ju, Climbing the Pagoda at the Temple of Compassion

The pagoda seems to burst from the earth,
reaching solitary and high into the heavens.
Climbing to the top, we leave the world behind,
the steps winding endlessly into the void.
So imposing it could command the whole country,
so tall, as if not built by human hands,
its four corners blot out the sun,
its seven stories reach to the sky.
We can look down on high-flying birds;
we hear the sound of a frightening wind.
Mountains roll into the distance like waves,
as if flowing eastward on the ebbing tide.
Green scholar trees crowd the Emperor's Road;
how marvelous are his palaces and halls.
Autumn colors come in from the west;
a gray haze fills the central plain.
To the north remain the Five Imperial Tombs,
green in the mist for all eternity.
Only now do I begin to understand
truths the sages struggled to attain.
I will put aside the trappings of my office,
to follow the Way and seek enlightenment.

GW

Yuan Jie

To the Tax Collectors, After the Bandits Withdrew

In the year 763, bandits from Xiyuan entered Daozhou to burn, kill and pillage, only leaving when almost nothing remained. The following year they came back and attacked Yongzhou, destroying the town of Shao, but then left without menacing this prefecture a second time. Was it because we were strong enough to defeat them? Of course not! It was because they pitied us. So how is it that *you* have the audacity to come back now and extort such ruinous taxes? This poem is for you.

Our world was once a peaceful place,
twenty tranquil years of hills and forests.
A spring flowed in my courtyard;
a deep ravine lay opposite my gate.
Taxes were collected in their season;
fearing nothing, people could sleep late.
Then, in an instant, all was changed;
for many years we lived with swords and banners.
When I was appointed Prefect here,
bandits from Xiyuan came to trouble us.
Our town is small, the bandits didn't kill us;
was it because the people are so poor?
Instead, they pillaged other nearby towns,
sparing us this time.
Now, following the Imperial command,
have you less compassion than bandits?
With these oppressive, cruel taxes,
you may as well be burning us alive.
How can you ruin people's lives this way,
just to flaunt your zeal for public duty?
I'm thinking of resigning as Prefect,
taking my little boat and drifting off.
I'll feed my family on fish and grain,
and grow old wandering rivers and lakes.

GW

Wei Yingwu

Literary Men Gather in My Prefecture on a Rainy Day

Outside, soldiers stand on guard with halberds,
inside this banquet hall, a balm of incense.
Wind and rain, carried in from the sea,
amply cool pavilion and lake.
All frets and fevers are soon dispelled,
as welcome guests begin to fill the hall.

I'm ashamed to live in this grand residence
when others' lives are so unsettled,
so let's not bother with formalities,
forget the customary protocols.

Although fresh meat is forbidden by decree,
there's fruit and vegetables to be enjoyed.
Bowing to each other, let's take a cup of wine,
look up and share our poems and responses.
A joyful spirit surely frees the body,
urging it to soar and circle with the wind.

Here in this province, literature is flourishing;
today we have talent gathered in abundance.
Now we have proved that, in this great land,
there are higher aims than reaping wealth and taxes.

MEF

Setting Off on the Yangzi, for Editor Yuan Jie

Sadly, I take leave of my dear friend,
as he floats into the mist that hugs the river.
My boat will take me onward to Luoyang,
behind me, the faint dawn bell from Guangling.
This morning, we had to say farewell;

when will we be together again?
Our lives are like this boat, borne on the waves,
against the current, or with it, never at rest.

G W

Sent to the Daoist Master on All Pepper Mountain

A touch of cold this morning in the District Office,
and suddenly I thought of you, up on your mountain,
gathering a bundle of firewood by the creek,
taking it home to boil white stones.
I thought of bringing you a jug of wine
to share on a night of wind and rain,
but falling leaves have filled the empty hills;
how could I have found the traces of your trail?

G W

Encountering Feng Zhu in the Capital

A traveler comes from the east,
his clothes still wet with Baling rain.
I ask him why he's come:
"To buy an axe for cutting firewood in the mountains."
Now flowers open, down among the fallen leaves;
swallow hatchlings struggle with the breeze.
Since we parted last year, spring has come again,
along with more white hair at our temples.

G W

Overnight at Xuyi

We lowered our sails to stop at Linhuai,
mooring by a deserted post station.
Then a giant wind raised such billows

that they blotted out the sunset.
People returned to the mountains in darkness;
geese flew down to the island of white rushes.
Alone at night, I think of the doors of home,
as I hear the bell, another sleepless traveler.

G W

East of the City

Trapped in my office all year long,
I've come out into sunlit countryside.
Willows dance in a lovely breeze;
green hills put my mind at ease.
I rest among some trees a while,
return to walk beside a blue stream.
There's mist and drizzle out there on the plain;
a turtle dove calls from somewhere out of sight.
It's so relaxing here, I would stay longer,
but unfinished work still beckons me.
I should finally retire and build a cabin,
to live like Tao Yuanming, my idol.

MEF

Farewell to My Daughter, Leaving to Marry into the Yang Clan

You've been so sad as this day approached;
you have such a long way to go, alone.
My daughter, now you will be married,
carried upstream in a tiny boat on this great river.
I'm sorry you had to grow up without your mother;
I tried to love you twice as much.
You helped me raise your little sister;
as you leave her, the two of you can't stop crying.
It's a sight that ties my insides up in knots.

It is right that you should go; how could I hold you back?
Since you were little, you missed what mothers teach;
I'm worried—will you treat your husband's mother with respect?
But, you join a family of good people;
I'm sure they will love you and keep you from mistakes.
We are poor, and poverty made us frugal;
I'm sorry your dowry had to be so modest.
Be filial and polite the way a woman should,
in speech and action, as I tried to teach you.
As you leave us on this morning,
I wonder which autumn will I see you next.
I can cope with disappointment on ordinary days,
but now, sadness overwhelms me;
as I walk home, watching your little sister,
tears quietly soak the ribbons of my cap.

G W

Liu Zongyuan

Early in the Morning, Reading a Buddhist Text at Master Zhao's Temple

Drawing icy water from the well, to cleanse my mouth,
focusing my mind, brushing dust from my robe,
I'm carrying a precious manuscript
as I leave the Eastern Temple, reading as I go.

This fountainhead has been neglected;
people forget what they're truly searching for.
The words are guides to deeper understanding,
but why are they so hard to master?

In the quiet of this temple courtyard
moss lends color to the dark bamboo.
The sun rises through lingering mist and dew,
green pine trees shine as if newly washed.

Untroubled now, I leave all words behind;
the heart's awareness is enough.

MEF

Dwelling Beside a Stream

Forever tied by the official hat-pin and seal-cord,
now it seems fortunate this southern barbarian was banished.
I stroll at leisure among the farmers' fields,
looking exactly like a rustic from the hills.
At dawn the farmers' plows turn the dewy grass;
at night oars clatter in the rocky stream.
Rambling around, I encounter no one;
I sing long songs to the blue skies of Chu.

DL

樂府
Five-Word Old-Style Yuefu

Wang Changling

Song of the Border (1)

Crickets chirp in the bare mulberry grove,
in the eighth month on the Xiao Pass road.
We go beyond the pass, and then return—
nothing there but withered reeds and grasses.
Troops, sent from their homes to the inner plains,
grow old out here in this sandy waste.
Pay no attention to those dashing cavalrymen,
always bragging about their fabulous horses.

G W

Song of the Border (2)

Crossing the river in autumn I stop to water my horse;
the water is cold and the wind like a knife.
The sun is not quite down over the flat desert sands,
and I see Lin Tau black against evening gloom.
In yesteryear's battles before the Long Wall,
they say the troops were eager, full of high spirits.
Only the yellow dust is eternal—
white bones lie scattered everywhere among the bushes.

D L

Li Bai

Moon over the Mountain Passes

A bright moon rises at the Heavenly Mountain
from an endless sea of clouds.
A long wind, from ten thousand miles away,
blows to us through the Jade Gate Pass.
Han troops descended the road to Mount Baideng;
Tartars coveted the shores of Koko Nor.
This place has always been a battleground,
and few have ever made it out alive.
Soldiers look across this vast borderland,
and think of going home, their faces bitter.
Back in high towers, under this very moon,
their wives have found no rest from endless sorrow.

GW

Four Songs of the Seasons in the Style of Zi Ye:

Spring

In the land of Qin, the lovely Luo Fu
gathers mulberry leaves beside clear water,
pale hands clutching green twigs,
fresh complexion rosy in the sun.
The silkworms are hungry, I have to go, sir,
don't linger here in that five-horse carriage!

Summer

At Mirror Lake (three hundred li across),
lotus buds are bursting into bloom.
In the fifth month, Xi Shi comes to pluck them;
crowds have gathered on the shore to watch.
Her boat turns back before the moon appears;
she hurries to the palace and her impatient King.

Autumn

A slice of moon above the capital;
washboards busy in ten thousand homes.
The autumn wind is blowing without let-up,
carrying our thoughts towards Jade Pass.
When will the Barbarians be defeated
and our good men come marching home again?

Winter

The messenger leaves tomorrow at first light;
all night, she sews a heavy cotton robe.
Her pale hands ply the ice-cold needle;
how can she bear to hold the scissors?
The task complete, she sends it on its journey.
Will it ever reach him at the far frontier?

MEF

A Song of Changgan

When my hair first covered my forehead,
I picked flowers and played with them by my gate.
You came, riding on a bamboo horse,
and played with plums around the railing of the well.
We both lived in Changan village,
two children with no suspicion of each other.
At fourteen, I became your wife;
I was shy, and had not yet smiled at you.
I lowered my head toward the shaded wall;
you called a thousand times, but I never answered.
At fifteen, I first began to smile,
and hoped we would be together, even as dust or ashes.
I believed we would never be apart,
so why would I ever need to climb the lookout tower?
When I was sixteen, you went on a long journey,
through Qutang Gorge with its Yanyu rocks,
sharp beneath the high water of the fifth month,
where the sad cries of the apes fill the skies.
By the front gate, your footprints are still there,
but one by one they fill with moss,
moss so deep now, I can't sweep it away,
as leaves fall early in autumn winds.
In the eighth month, butterflies have come;
pairs of them flutter in our western garden.
Seeing these things makes my heart sad;
I sit, mourning the loss of my youthful beauty.
When, at last, you set out from the Three Gorges,
send a letter ahead to let me know.
I will come to meet you, no matter how far,
even all the way to Long Wind Sands.

GW

Meng Jiao

Song of a Virtuous Woman

Wutong trees grow old with branches intertwined;
mandarin ducks mate for life, then die together.
A faithful wife, after her husband dies,
should give up her life, just as they do.
Waves I promise will never rise,
my heart stilled, like water in a well.

G W

Song of a Traveling Son

Thread in the hand of a loving mother:
a coat her son will wear far away.
He is leaving soon; her stitches grow smaller and smaller,
her heart sick that he must leave so soon, be gone so long.
How can a one-inch blade of grass,
repay the kindness of three long months of spring?

GW

七言古詩
Seven-Word Old-Style Poems

Chen Ziang

Song on Climbing the Terrace at Youzhou

Before me, I cannot see the men of ages gone;
after me, I cannot see those yet to come.
Struck by the vast emptiness of Heaven and earth,
alone, sick at heart, my tears begin to fall.

GW

Li Qi

In an Antique Style

These men are veterans of long marches;
though young, they have fought in Youzhou and in Yan.
They risk their all under enemy horses' hooves,
caring nothing for their own lives.
In battle, they kill their foes, who dare not advance,
frightened by their whiskers, stiff as hedgehog quills.

Their horses fly like white clouds under yellow clouds of dust;
till they requite a nation's favor, they will not return to their homes.

Here in Liaodong, a young girl barely fifteen,
master of the lute and matchless as singer and dancer,
plays a frontier tune for us on her Tibetan flute,
and three armies' tears fall down like rain.

GW

Farewell to Chen Zhangfu

The fourth month: wind from the south, barley tall and golden,
date-flowers not yet tumbled, wutong leaves grown long.
Those hills we left this morning are still in view at sunset;
the horses whinnied all the way, thinking of home.

Chen, my noble friend, you're a man of honor,
with your dragon beard, tiger eyebrows, lofty forehead.
You've swallowed and digested ten thousand books,
and refused to lower your head among the nation's weeds.

At the east gate, you brought your colleagues wine;
we viewed all things with glad hearts, light as swans' feathers.
Reclining drunk, not knowing the time of day,
now and then we'd watch a cloud pass high above.

On the great river, waves are reaching to the dark sky;
the boat rests in the ferry dock, unable to cross.
Travelers to Zheng can't reach their homes,
and Luoyang people voice frustrated sighs.

I heard that in your circle you had many friends:
yesterday you lost your post; where are those friends today?

MEF

Song of a Lute

Our host has wine; a pleasant evening is ensured;
he's invited a fine musician to play the *Guangling San.*
Moonrise at the city wall; a few crows are flying;
frost has gripped ten thousand trees; wind cuts through our robes.
With a bronze stove burning, candles add more light
as he begins to play *Clear Stream* then *Consort Chu.*
One note and already all the world is hushed;
guests listen, rapt, as stars slowly fade away.
My orders are to travel onward, a thousand miles to Huai;
dare I tell them clouds and mountains mark my journey's end?

MEF

On Hearing Dong Tinglan Play the Tune "The Sound of the Tartar Reed-flute." Sent to Supervising Secretary Fang

Long ago, Cai Yan wrote her "Song of the Tartar Reed-flute;"
in all, it made up eighteen stanzas.
Hearing it, Tartars cried till their tears drenched the frontier grass,
and the Han emissaries' hearts broke as they waited to take her home,
imagining the old ramparts deserted and signal fires cold,
the white snow flying in that endless wasteland.
Now, he plucks the *shang* note, then *jiao* and *yu,*
and all around us, autumn leaves rustle in reply.

O Master Dong,
how great your genius!
From deep in the mountains, spirits come to listen in the shadows.
Slow notes, then fast as the strings answer your hand;
the music, as it ebbs and flows, seems to be pure emotion.
On empty mountains, a hundred birds scatter, then roost;
the thousand miles of floating clouds, now dark, now bright.
The mournful cry of a young goose, flying lost in the night sky,
or the sobbing of a mother, cut off from her sons, far off among the
    Tartars.
The river's waves are stilled,
and birds stop their chatter.
From a barbarian village, thoughts of home far away;
in the sand and dust of Lhasa, a sad fate lamented.

Then, the somber key changes, and a breeze fresh with rain
blows through the forest, drops rattling on roof tiles;
spray from a spring flies into treetops,
and a wild deer barks, trotting past the hall.

East of the Changan palace, by the Chancellery wall,
your office faces the Phoenix Pool and the blue lacquer gates.

Though a great talent, you care nothing for fame or high office,
day and night watching only for him to come, carrying his lute.

GW

Listening to An Wanshan Play His Reed Whistle

On South Mountain, he cut bamboo to make his whistle.
This music originally came from Kucha.
After it came to the land of Han, its sound was unique.
This tartar from Liangzhou plays it for me.

The bystanders hear it and sigh endlessly;
travelers far from home are all moved to tears.
People hear it but don't appreciate what they hear;
its tone is like a howling, spinning storm,

like withered mulberry or old cypress trees sighing in a cold wind,
or nine phoenix chicks confusedly chirping,
or dragons bellowing and tigers screaming at the same time.
Then every sound of nature, a hundred bubbling springs, all fall
    silent.

Suddenly, it changes to the tune of Yuyang drums;
yellow clouds grow lonely and the sun fades to dark.
Then, changed again, it is like "Willows in Spring"
as if every flower in the Shanglin Gardens bloomed at once.

On New Year's Eve, in the high hall, bright candles burn in rows.
For each cup of fine wine, there's another marvelous tune.

GW

Meng Haoran

Song: Returning to Deer Gate at Night

A temple bell sounds as dusk approaches.
Fisher-folk clamor as they jostle for the ferry;
others walk the sand-path to the river village.
I too ride the boat as far as Deer Gate.

At Deer Gate, moonlight cuts through mist around the trees,
and suddenly, I've reached the place of Hermit Pang.
The cliff-side door, the path through pines, now desolate;
few traces of the hermit who once passed back and forth.

MEF

Li Bai

A Ballad of Mount Lu; Sent to Censor Lu Xuzhou

I'm just like the Madman of Chu,
singing my "Phoenix Song" to mock Confucius.
My hand grasps the green jade staff,
as I set out at dawn from the Yellow Crane Tower,
off to the Five Peaks, in search of Immortals, no matter how far;
my whole life, I've loved to visit mountains.
Mount Lu, in its glory, rises as the pass to the Southern Bushel;
its flanks glow, embroidered by clouds, a ninefold screen beneath
    the Five Peaks,
whose shadows fall on the lake shining in green light,
where Censer Peak and Twin Swords stand face to face,
there before the golden Stone Gate Mountain.
Rivers like the Milky Way pour down beneath three stone bridges,
meeting at the great cascade beneath the Censer.
All around cliffs rise in broad spreading layers of mist.
Green shadows and rosy clouds glow in the sunrise;
in the vast sky, no single bird is flying.
I climb high between heaven and earth for this grand view,
the Yangzi flowing endlessly away.
Yellow clouds, borne ten thousand miles on the wind, change the
    color of the sky,
the waterfall now like a snowy mountain with nine torrents
    running down.

I wrote this Ballad of Mount Lu,
inspired by the presence of this mountain.
At leisure, I looked in a stone mirror, and my heart grew still;
Xie Lingyun also came here, but his footprints are lost beneath the
    moss.

I have taken cinnabar to leave all thought of the world behind,
hoping a harmonious spirit would bring me closer to the Dao.

I can see the Immortals far off on their particolored clouds,
holding lotus flowers as they enter the Jade Emperor's palace.
So come meet me some time, to wander emptiness beyond the
    Nine Heavens,
and we will travel the universe as Lu Ao did of old.

GW

My Dream of Visiting Mount Tianyu

Seafaring men will tell you of the Land of the Immortals
that can never be reached through mists and massive waves;
the people of Yue tell stories of the Lady of the Heavens:
sometimes she'll reveal herself through shifting clouds and rainbows.
The Heavenly Lady reaches out to touch the sky,
higher than the Sacred Mountains, obscuring cities
with mile after mile of sky terrace
sloping down towards the southeast.

In my dream, I longed to go to Wu and Yue,
flying over Mirror Lake by moonlight,
my shadow on the lake below.
Arriving at Shan Creek,
the old Xie lodge was still there
with green water, gibbons howling.
At the lodge I put on straw sandals
to climb the stairway to the sky.
I could see half the country and the sunlit sea
and heard a cock crow overhead.

Among endless ravines and pathless cliffs,
admiring the flowers, I leaned on a boulder
and didn't notice darkness closing in.
Bears roared, dragons groaned, among the dark red cliffs and springs.
The deep forest trembled, the mountain peak crumbled,
dark clouds gathered, threatening rain,
mist spread over roiling water.
Columns opened up to thunderbolts,

72

the whole mountain chain was heaving.
Stones of the Heavenly Gateway tumbled;
with deafening noise, the center opened up
a vast and bottomless chasm.

Then sun and moon lit up the gold and silver terrace.
There, in rainbow clothes, riding on the wind,
dwellers in the clouds were gathering:
lute-playing tigers, chariots drawn by phoenix-birds,
immortals lined in rows, like fields of hemp.

Suddenly, I jumped in terror at this vision,
gasped and sighed in deep confusion.
Slowly I came to realize
pillow and cover were those clouds and mists.

This is always the way with human pleasure:
Ten Thousand Things beyond our reach
are carried off like water flowing east.

Leaving: my friend, who knows when I'll return?
White deer live in freedom on a green slope;
I must hurry off to that great mountain.
To stay here, bow and scrape to those in power,
would surely damage my integrity.

MEF

Farewell at a Wine-shop in Jinling

Wind blows the willows and fills the shop with fragrance;
Wu girls bring wine and urge their guests to drink.
All my friends in Jinling have come to say farewell;
it is time to go, but I won't till every cup is empty.
I ask you, friends, as the water flows east,
which is longer, our sadness or this river?

GW

At Xie Tiao Tower in Xuanzhou, a Farewell Feast for Secretary Shu Yun

I've given up on yesterday,
since it abandoned me.
Now I face today's new troubles
with a troubled heart.

Strong winds bear the autumn wild goose
away to far-off places;
from this high tower,
I can only down my wine and watch.

Your vivid writings bring to mind the Jianan style
and express too, the spirit of Xie Tiao,
encompassing the bold and brilliant,
urging us to soar to heaven, touch the moon.

Slice water with a sword? It still flows on.
Drink to drown your sorrow? Sorrow wins.
Life in this world can never match our dreams;
tomorrow, I'll loose my hair, step in my boat and sail away.

MEF

Cen Shen

A Ballad of Running Horse Creek, Composed for Grand Master Feng Changqing as He Takes His Army Westward

Have you not seen, Sir,
Running Horse Creek flowing beside an ocean of snow,
the vast desert stretching off, yellow as far as Heaven?

In the ninth month, at Wheel Terrace, the wind howls at night;
the creek is full of broken stones as big as bushels;
blown on the wind, scattered, smaller stones fly everywhere.

When the Tartar grass turned yellow, and their horses fat and
    sleek,
from Gold Mountain, their dust and smoke rose in the west,
so the great general of Han leads his army west to meet them.

The general wears his golden armor through the night;
at midnight, his men march, their spears clashing,
the wind like a knife, slashing their faces.

Their horses' tails are full of snow, their sweat boiling like steam,
then freezing into ice on the manes of these great chargers,
as in your tent, you draft a declaration, the ink freezing as you
    write.

When they hear your words, then they will know terror,
and dare not come to cross swords with you.
We will wait at the west gate for word of your great victory.

GW

A Song of Wheel Terrace, Composed for Grand Master Feng Changqing as He Takes His Army Westward

Atop the walls of Wheel Terrace, a bugle in the night;
north of the walls of Wheel Terrace, the Pleiades are setting.

An urgent message arrived last night, come through Quli;
the Chanyu have reached the slope of Gold Mountain!

From the watchtowers, we look west toward their dust in the
    darkness,
and at the Han army already camped north of Wheel Terrace.

Our General hoists his flag and leads his army west;
by dawn tomorrow, the whole army will be on the march.

From every direction, the thunder of drums, the ocean of snow is
    roiled;
three armies cheer as one, shaking the Shadow Mountains.

Beyond the Tartar borders, our martial spirit rises to the clouds;
on the battlefield, abandoned bones lie tangled in the grass.

Harsh winds over Sword River fill the air with snow;
at Shakou frozen rocks threaten, hooves are lost to frostbite.

In service to the Throne, our General welcomes any hardship;
he swore an oath to pacify the borders.
Who has not read the annals of former times?
The glory you earn now surpasses all.

                                                                    G W

A Song of Snow: Farewell to Administrative Assistant Wu, Returning to the Capital

A north wind rolled across the plain, killing the pasture grass;
in the eighth month, Tartar skies were filled with snow,
as if spring's breath had come one night,
with ten million pear trees breaking into blossom.
It blew through pearl screens, melted on silk curtains;
no warmth in fox-fur coats, or under brocade quilts.
The General's inlaid bow was so cold he could not draw it;
the Marshall's steel armor froze to his skin.
Ice covered this vast desert a hundred yards deep;
gloomy clouds darkened ten thousand frigid miles.

The General laid a feast to toast your transfer home,
with frontier music: Tartar lutes and nomad flutes.
A blinding snow at evening cloaked the headquarters gate;
strong winds shook red banners frozen stiff.

I see you off from the East Gate at Luntai;
snow has blocked all routes through the Heavenly Mountains.
The road bends around hills and soon you will disappear,
leaving your horse's hoof prints behind you as you go.

G W

Du Fu

At Office Manager Wei Feng's House, I Saw a Painting of Horses by General Cao Ba

Since the founding of our nation, of all who painted horses,
the greatest by far was the Prince of Jiangdu.
But then came General Cao, who, after thirty years of a warrior's
    fame,
gave the world again some truly shining steeds.

He painted the former Emperor's luminous mount,
and thunder crashed for ten days above the Dragon Pool.
In the Palace Treasury, there was a dark red agate plate,
Ladies of Handsome Fairness passed the word for Ladies of Talents
    to find it.

Presented with the plate, the General paid deep homage and went
    home;
white silks and sheer satins followed him there one after another.
The noble and the powerful all commissioned paintings,
and began to see their screens and panels shine with dazzling light.

From the old days, Taizong's horse "Tan Curls,"
and later times, Guo Ziyi's "Lion Flower,"
both are in his latest painting.
Once again, the connoisseurs cannot stop their sighing.
On any of these horses, one cavalryman could defeat ten thousand.
Beneath his brush white silk has become the frontier's windswept
    desert.

The other seven horses are also splendid steeds;
in the distance, a cold sky blends with mist and snow.
Frosted hooves kick the long road between catalpas;
grooms and servants stand in rows like forest trees.
Marvel how these nine horses, in spirited competition,

lift their heads high, with dignity and pride.
Who, you may ask, most deeply loves, best knows these horses?
In our days, Wei Feng; before him Zhi Dun.

I remember, when the Emperor traveled to the Xingfeng Palace,
kingfisher banners brushed the sky as they traveled east.
Prancing in a great mass, thirty thousand horses,
each one, a painted image come to life.
When funeral gifts were offered to the River Gods
heroic deeds like water-dragon hunts were ended.
Don't you see, sir,
the Golden Tomb is overgrown with pine and cypress,
all traces of His Court are gone; only birds cry in the wind.

GW

A Song of Painting: to General Cao Ba

You, General, descended from Emperor Wu of Wei,
now live as a peasant, a cold-door commoner.
Although that heroic age of conquest is long over,
its cultural brilliance still survives in your work.
To learn calligraphy, you first studied with Lady Wei;
your only regret was not surpassing great Wang Xizhi.
You say, "Caught up in my painting, I give no thought to old age;
riches and rank to me are no more than clouds floating by."

Often summoned to court during the Kaiyuan period,
you frequently ascended the dais to receive the Emperor's praise.
In the gallery of Famous Men, the noble faces were fading;
going to work with your brush, you made them bright again.
On the ministers' heads, you repainted their hats of office,
at the waists of fierce generals, their great feathered arrows.
The Duke of Bao and Duke of E—so lifelike their hair bristles—
stand grim, bold and heroic, as if still drunk with battle.
The late Emperor's dappled horse, Jade-Flower,
was painted by artist after artist: none captured his likeness.

79

One day he was led into the courtyard below the red steps;
just standing, he brought with him the wind of the plains.
At the Emperor's command, you stretched white silk;
calling up all of your skill, you formed the image in your mind.
In a flash, from the nine-fold heavens, the true dragon appeared!
At one stroke, the horse paintings of ages were obliterated.

When the painting was taken up and hung behind the throne,
the horse on the wall, and that in the court, stood facing each
    other.
Smiling, the Emperor urged his aide to bring a reward;
stable boys and grooms stood about long-faced with envy.
Your pupil Han Gan was shown all of your techniques;
he too can paint horses, horses in every stance imaginable,
but Gan paints only the outer flesh, not the strong frame beneath.
His brush would sap the spirit of legendary Hualiu!

The General is a superb painter because he captures the essence.
In the past you also made portraits, but only of exceptional men;
in the present troubled times, uprooted and homeless,
you are reduced to painting portraits of humble passersby.
So desperate are your straits, you suffer dirty looks from vulgar
    eyes.
Perhaps never in the world has a gentleman been poor as you!

But look at the lives of those in history rich in fame—
many among them also dealt with endless frustrations.

DL

Sent to Grand Master of Remonstrance Han Zhu

Today, I am unhappy, to think of you down in Yueyang.
I would fly to you, but instead I am sick in bed,
separated from you, in your retirement, by this autumn water,
as you wash your feet in Lake Dongting and look into the
    distance.

Geese fly by, high in the sky, lit by sun and moon.
Green sweetgum leaves turn red as autumn frosts begin.
All the spirits in heaven are gathering around the Big Dipper,
some riding unicorns, some mounted on phoenix.
Hibiscus flower flags wave and drift down through misty air;
their shadows cover the flowing water of southern rivers.
In the heavenly palace, all are drunk on precious liquor.
True sages are now rare at Court; like you, most have withdrawn.
I recall that recluse of former days, Master Red Pine,
probably the same man as Zhang Liang of the Han era.
Earlier, he was at Liu Bang's side when they pacified Changan,
but his strategic plan was not followed, so he became disillusioned.
In the end, he could do nothing about the rise and fall of nations,
so he became an ascetic and lived on sweetgum sap.
We have always pitied Sima Tan's having been left behind at
     Zhounan.
May the stars grant longer life to you, another Sima Tan.
O my old friend, why are you separated from me by the autumn
     flood?
If only I could take you to Changan as a gift to the Imperial
     Court.

                                                    G W

The Ancient Cypress

In front of Gongming Temple stands an ancient cypress.
Its boughs are like bronze, its roots hard as stone.
Its age-hoared, rain-washed bark circles a trunk forty spans thick;
its jet-black branches meet the sky two thousand feet up!
The ruler and his minister have lived out their time,
but this tree is still cherished by people of today.
When clouds come, they join it to mists rising from long Wu
     Gorge;
at moonrise, it feels the same chill as the snow-covered mountains.
I recall where the road winds east around my Brocade pavilion,
past the temple shared by Liu Bei and his martial Marquis.

There too were cypresses whose branches lofted high above the
     ancient plain
and hung over the secluded temple, its faded paint and staring
     windows.
But this tree, with its python roots, manages to hold itself upright
despite the battering winds in the high, lonely depths of the sky.
Only the power of a divine spirit could hold it so tall and straight—
its lofty height makes manifest the Creator's own hand!
If a great Hall had collapsed and needed rafters and beams,
the thousands of ox teams would balk, turning to stare at the
     mountainous weight.
Even without the carving of craftsmen it is already a wonder of the
     world;
it has never resisted the axe—there is simply no way to haul it off.
The bitter heart may be unable to resist the ravaging termites,
but still its aromatic leaves sustain the roosting Phoenix.
Men of ambition, you who labor unnoticed, don't sigh with
     resentment—
from of old, towering timber has been hard to make use of.

DL

A Ballad: Watching a Pupil of Miss Gongsun the First Perform the Sword Dance

On the nineteenth day of the tenth month of the second year of the Dali era,
at the house of Yuan Chi, Administrative Aide at Kuizhou, I watched Miss Li
the Twelfth of Linying perform the Sword Dance. I so appreciated her exquisite
dancing, I asked her who her teacher had been. She replied, "I studied with
Miss Gongsun the First." In the third year of the Kaiyuan era, when I was still
a boy, I remember seeing Miss Gongsun perform the Sword Dance and the
Felt Hat Dance at Yancheng. The freedom and spontaneity of her dancing were
the finest of her day. In the early years of the former Emperor, among all the
women of the Welcoming Spring or Pear Garden Imperial dancing schools, or
other dancers occasionally invited to the palace, who performed before him,
Miss Gongsun was the only one able to perform these dances. Gradually her
beauty faded, just as my hair turned white. Even this woman, her student, is

no longer young. Having settled the question of origins, knowing their styles were the same, and overcome with emotion about these events in the past, I wrote this "Ballad of the Sword Dance." Long ago, Zhang Xu of Wu was a master at the cursive calligraphy style. Many times, he saw Miss Gongsun the First perform the West River Sword Dance at Yexian. After that, his cursive style became even more beautiful, with a lofty spirit and a profound sense of movement, influenced by the great art of Miss Gongsun.

Long ago, there was a beautiful woman named Gongsun,
whose Sword Dance moved the four quarters of the world.
A mountain of spectators watched her in amazement;
heaven and earth rose and fell, following her motion.
Light flashed from her sword, as when great Yi shot the nine suns
    down;
her graceful leaps were flying Immortals mounted on dragons.
When she began, drums sounded with the fury of thunder;
when she ended, light reflected from the frozen sea of faces.
Then, her pink lips were silent and her pearl sleeves were stilled;
now her masterful dancing lives on only in her student.
The beauty from Linying, here at the White Emperor City,
sings and dances with ascendant genius.
In my question and her answer were the key to her art,
and I ponder sadly the turn of our life and times.

The late Emperor had eighty thousand women in his palace;
at the Sword Dance, among them all, Miss Gongsun ranked first.
Fifty years have passed in the flick of a hand;
the dust of war has darkened the Imperial Palace.
The students of the Pear Garden have been scattered like mist;
only this woman remains, alone in the chill of dusk.
The trees on the Bright Emperor's tomb are already tall;
and I am here in the Qutang Gorge where the grass has withered.
After the banquet, as its stirring music stills,
joy already fades as the crescent moon rises.
I am an old man, not knowing where I'm going next,
but moss grows beneath my feet, I must head into the mountains.

GW

Yuan Jie

Drinking Song at Stonefish Lake with an Introduction

Everywhere old men brew wine with rice from public fields. In my leisure time I took some wine to the lake and enjoyed the chance to get drunk on the shore. We could reach out, buy more wine from the wine boats for us to sit and drink. We were at Ba Island, with Jun Mountain looming above us. Even when the waves were huge, the wine boats could reach us. I composed this song to celebrate.

Stonefish Lake is like Dongting,
with rising summer waters, Jun Mountain turning green.
The mountain, a winejar; the lake, a pool of wine.
We drinking men are gathered along the island sands.

Strong winds for days on end stir massive waves,
but they haven't stopped the boatmen bringing wine.
With a huge wine-gourd in my hands, I sit on Ba Island
dispensing wine for all of us to drink away our sorrows.

MEF

Han Yu

Mountain Rocks

Jagged mountain crags, narrow pathways:
at twilight as I reached the temple, bats were flying.
I climbed to the hall, sat down on rain-washed steps
among great plantain leaves, swollen jasmine buds.

The priest informed me of a splendid Buddha painting;
he brought a light to show me; I could see it was unique.
He spread my bed, shook the mat, prepared soup and rice:
coarse food, but good enough to satisfy my hunger.
Late that night I lay in stillness, insects silent now;
the moon rose above the ridge, shining through my door.

When daylight came, I left without a path to follow,
wandered here and there through heavy mist.
Red peaks, jade streams, one after another, brimming over—
at last I came to pines and oaks, all of massive span.
Barefoot, I trod on stones to cross the streams,
water gurgling, breezes blowing wide my robe.

If life could remain like this, a person could be happy—
why are we always tethered to officialdom?
A few close friends might get together,
settle here, find peace in our old age.

MEF

On Mid-Autumn Night, Given to Administrator Zhang Shu of the Personnel Evaluation Section

Fine clouds in every direction, the River of Stars was hidden;
A light breeze scattered moonlight on the ripples.
Smooth sand, no reflections in the still water.
I offered you a cup of wine: your turn to sing.

Your song was sad and tinged with bitterness,
Before you finished, my tears fell like rain:

"Lake Dongting stretches to the horizon, Mount Jiuyi stands tall;
dragons surface, then dive; apes and flying foxes wail.
Nine out of ten would have died on the hard road to this post;
we live in such obscurity here, we may as well be dead.
Getting out of bed afraid of snakes, at meals afraid of being
    poisoned;
the air is so dank, everything stinks of mildew.
It seems like only yesterday, they beat the great drum at the county
    seat,
announcing a new emperor upon the throne, needing wise
    ministers.

Word came of amnesty, three thousand miles in one day;
even death sentences were commuted.
Those demoted might return, those banished might go home;
those who had polluted the Court were gone, only the pure
    remained.
Then we applied for reinstatement, but our superiors blocked it;
we were sent deeper into the unwholesome south.
Our new titles were so modest we couldn't bear to pronounce them;
in such posts as we keep, mistakes are punished by flogging in the
    dust.
Those banished with us were almost all on the homeward road,
a road that's out of reach for us, impossible to climb."

Sir, please end your song and listen to mine;
my song has a different theme from yours:

"In a whole year, how many nights with such a moon?
Our lives are determined by fate, not by other men.
We have wine: let us drown our sorrows in this moonlight."

GW

Visiting Mount Heng, I Stayed Overnight at Yue Temple and Inscribed This on the Gate Archway

The Five Sacred Mountains are as honored as the Three Dukes;
Song Mountain holds the center, guarded by the other four.
Here in this fiery southern place, wild enough for ghosts and
    demons,
local spirits carry heaven-granted special powers.
Swirling clouds and clinging mists half conceal the torso;
there has to be a summit, but who had ever seen it?

I arrived right in the autumn rainy season,
gloomy weather, overcast, with no fresh winds.
My silent praying seemed to find an answer—
wasn't this divine response to honesty and virtue?
Suddenly the clouds around the peak were swept away;
looking up, I saw the column buttressing the blue void.
The Purple Canopy was linked to the Celestial Pillar,
the Stone Granary leaped toward the God of Fire.
Deep in awe, I dismounted, offered up a prayer,
then rushed past pine and cypress to the temple.

Wall after wall, crimson columns shining,
images of spirits, demons, garish red and blue.
I climbed the steps, offered up dried meat and wine,
hoping my sincerity excused such meager gifts.
The old priest of the temple was acquainted with the spirits:
with a piercing stare, he sized me up and, bowing low,
took a bowl of divination discs, showed me how to cast them,
assured me that their pattern was by far the most auspicious.

Although I'm exiled in barbarian lands, my fortune hasn't faded:
I've simple food and clothes enough to meet my needs.
My hopes for worldly fame have long been set aside;
now I value hard-won blessings from the gods.

That night I lay in the temple's high pavilion.
The light of stars and moon was dimmed by dawn's light clouds.
Apes called, a bell sounded, reminding me that it was day;
then, over in the east, a cold bright sun appeared.

MEF

An Elegy for the Stone Drums

Zhang Ji held a rubbing from the stone drums in his hand,
and urged me to write an elegy for the drums.
Du Fu is no more among us, Li Bai is dead,
what can a modest talent like mine say about these famous drums?
When Zhou rule was collapsing, and the whole world boiled,
King Xuan rose in anger and his lance shook the world.
He opened wide the Bright Hall to the tribute of nations,
and so many lords came, their swords and girdle-stones clashed
    together.
To show his might, the King held a hunt on Mt. Qi's southern
    slope;
every beast and bird for a thousand miles was driven into his nets.
To engrave a record of his achievement that would last ten
    thousand ages,
they hewed stone into drums that were polished smooth.
His retainers were the finest scholars of their age,
their best poems were chosen, carved on the drums, and left on the
    mountain.
Rain scoured them, the sun baked them, wildfires burned them;
but spirits kept watch and protected them all these years.
Sir, where did you get this paper rubbing, I asked him,
so perfect, so true to each carved line and word?
Such austere phrases, their meanings obscure and difficult to read,

the characters neither scribal hand nor tadpole style.
After so many years, how have they not worn away?
The strokes are still vigorous, quick swords severing an alligator,
a phoenix dancing in the sky, a flock of immortals flying by,
or trees of lapis and coral with branches intertwined,
golden cords and iron hawsers tightly bound,
or an ancient ruler's cauldron, sunk in the river, or a dragon
  soaring on high.
The mediocre scholars who compiled the *Odes* did not include
  them;
their compass was too narrowly defined.
Confucius traveled west, but not as far as Qin,
so his collection, the *Odes*, included the stars, but ignored these,
  the sun and moon.
I love these antiques so much, why was I born too late?
Tears flow down my cheeks as I reach out to them.
I remember, I'd just won the highest degree,
it was the first year of the Yuanhe Reign.
An old friend was serving in the army at Fengxiang.
He helped me devise a plan to rescue the stone drums.
I purified myself and in clean cap and robes, approached the
  Chancellor and said,
"How few such precious things have been preserved!
They should be carefully wrapped in rugs and mats,
just a few camels could carry ten drums here.
Like the ritual cauldron of Gao now in the Temple of Confucius,
their value would increase beyond all measure.
If, by the Emperor's grace, they were to rest at the National
  College,
the students there could study them and thereby refine their
  learning.
When the Han carved the Classics on stone, scholars filled their
  gates,
so now the learned of the Empire would all flock here to see them.
We would scrape off the moss to expose the intricate carving,
then lay them in a suitable spot, on level ground.
Sheltered in a great hall with overhanging eaves,

they would be safe forever from further harm."
The Chancellor had served long by wisely avoiding decisions;
though he may have been moved, in the end he did nothing,
so shepherds still use them to strike fire, cattle to whet their horns.
Who is left to care for them with honor and respect?
Every day, every month, they decay as the earth reclaims them;
these six years I have looked westward, helpless and sorry.
Wang Xizhi's calligraphy, even tossed off, was beautiful,
but a few sheets could be had for the price of a goose.
These drums survived the wars of eight Dynasties;
what sense is there in neglecting them today?
The wars have ended and the world is at peace;
talented scholars are honored, Confucius and Mencius respected.
How is it, with such learned men in office,
that I can't persuade them, my voice grown weak?
So, I end my elegy for these great stone drums,
with a cry of despair at my utter failure.

GW

Liu Zongyuan

An Old Fisherman

An old fisherman spends the night by the West Cliff,
drawing water from the clear Xiang by firelight.

At sunrise, when the mist has cleared, he's nowhere to be seen,
ah, only a faint echo of oars among mountains and green water.

Looking back, all I see is water, flowing to the far horizon,
and heedless clouds above the cliff, drifting one by one.

MEF

Bai Juyi

The Song of Endless Sorrow

The Han Emperor craved women and sought a perfect beauty.
Years he ruled and yet he had not found her.
The Yang clan had a girl, just growing up;
raised in the women's quarters, few had seen her.
Such beauty, a gift of Heaven, should not be wasted.
On the day they brought her to the palace, our ruler first saw her.
A sidelong glance, a little smile, from this beauty,
and all the other women in six palaces came to nothing.

In the spring chill, they bathed her in the Huaqing pool;
the water of the warm springs glistened on her pale skin.
Her maids lifted her out, languid from the heat;
and there, for the first time, she received her master's favor.

Her hair was like clouds, in a golden headdress, her face a flower.
They passed spring nights, warm behind hibiscus curtains,
spring nights so bitterly short, and yet the sun rose high.
From that time on, he held no morning audience.

Endlessly they sought pleasure, at parties and banquets.
Endless love they sought in endless spring, night and night again.

In harem palaces, three thousand beauties,
but all were nothing, and one was everything.
In her golden room, her make-up perfect, she alone would serve him.
After banquets, in jade towers, wine fed their passion.

Her sisters and brothers were all ennobled.
Everyone envied the glory she brought to her clan,
until, through the world, parents' hearts
prayed for a daughter and not for a son.

Her new palaces rose on Mt. Li, touching the clouds,
and everywhere magical music drifted on the wind.

Softly she sang and softly she danced to the music of flute and
    strings.
Day after day the Emperor watched and listened, craving more.
But the sound of other music, martial drums, came from Yuyang,
    and it shook the earth,
ending her dance of the "Rainbow Dress" and the "Feathered Coat."

The nine-storied city gates were wrapped in smoke and dust
as a thousand chariots and ten thousand men rode out to the
    southwest.

His banners waved in the wind as they marched, and then stopped,
west of the Palace gates only thirty miles or so.
The Six Armies would go no farther, what could he do?
They dragged his beauty to her death beneath their horses.

Her flowery pin fell to the earth. No one retrieved it,
nor the jade and golden ornaments from her hair.
Her Emperor hid his face. He could not save her.
When finally he looked, her blood and tears had run together.

Yellow dust covered everything, blown on a mournful wind.
They climbed into clouds the winding Sword Peak Road.
When they passed below Emei Mountain, few watched them;
their flags were dark and dull in the fading light.

Shu rivers still ran blue; Shu mountains remained green.
Oblivious to all, grief filled his endless days and nights.
Moonlight in the borrowed palace only wrenched his heart the more.
On rainy nights, bells wrung his heart.

Time passed. At last he journeyed homeward,
but when he reached that spot again, he stopped, could not go on.
Below Mawei slope, into the muddy earth,
her pale face was gone, the scene of her death just emptiness.

Lord and Ministers eyed each other, robes soaked with tears.
Looking east toward the palace gates, their horses led them home.

They returned to find her ponds and gardens as before,
Lake Taiye hibiscus and Weiyang Palace willows.

The hibiscus like her face, the willows her eyebrows:
seeing all this, how could his tears not fall?
In spring wind, peach and plum both blossomed;
in fall rain, tung trees dropped their leaves.

Western Palace, Southern Hall grew thick with autumn grass;
red leaves fell and covered stairs where no one swept.
The actors and dancers of her Pear Garden all grew gray;
the eunuchs of her private suite aged like fading flowers.

At dusk, in his rooms, he shared his quiet thoughts with fireflies.
His single lamp flickered out; sleep could not find him.
Drums and bells tolled the hours slowly in the endless night,
till a gleam in the stars told dawn would come at last.

On nights so cold frost grayed the bright mandarin ducks on the
    roof tiles,
he was chill beneath the kingfisher quilt that none could share.
The living and the dead apart, a year went by,
and her ghost never came to him, even in dreams.

There was a Daoist from Linqiong then dwelling in the Capital.
Pure of heart, he could bring back souls from the dead, they said.
Moved by the Emperor's deep grief,
he sent his disciples to seek her in every quarter.

They rose into the sky and flew like lightning,
and soaring to the heavens, or deep under the earth,
gazed up into the endless blue, and deep as the Yellow Springs.
But both, they found empty. She was not there.

Then he heard of a magical island out in the eastern sea,
a mountain dividing nowhere from the very edge of nothing.

At its peak, magnificent towers rose into multicolored clouds.
There beautiful spirits lived eternities.
One was a woman called Most Faithful.
Snowy skin and lovely face, was she the one they sought?

He knocked on the jeweled door of her gold tower's western
    chamber,
and asked the maid Little Jade to announce him.
News of a heavenly envoy from Emperor of the Han
broke into her dreams as she slept within nine-flowered curtains.

Reaching for her gown, pushing away her pillow, she stood,
    unsteady,
and then, she parted her pearl curtains and her silver screen.
Just awake, her cloud-like hair was all disheveled;
her flowered headdress leaned askew as she came into the hall.

A breeze blew open her fairy cloak, it rippled and fluttered
as if she danced again the "Rainbow Dress" and the "Feathered
    Coat."
Her sad, lonely face was awash in tears,
like a sprig of pear blossoms, wet with the rain of spring again.

Touched, she met his eyes and thanked the Emperor for sending
    this envoy.
She said that since they had parted, she had never once heard his
    voice or seen his face.
No longer could they share their love, as in the Shining Palace;
alone here now in Paradise Hall, her days and months grew long.

Sometimes, she looked down into the world of the living,
but she never saw Changan, only the dust and fog of war that
    covered it.
Now, she offered two old tokens of her deepest feelings,

a case of silver filigree and a hairpin of gold, to send home with
    the envoy.

Of the pin, she kept half, of the case, one panel,
breaking the gold of the pin and splitting the silver of the case.
She prayed his love would last as long as the gold and silver,
so that someday, in heaven or on earth, they might meet again.

As the envoy left, she begged him also to carry back a message,
whose words were a vow that only they two would ever know.
On the seventh night of the seventh month, in the Palace of Long
    Life,
at midnight, they had promised, where none could overhear them:
"In the sky, we will be like birds with shared wings,
on earth, like trees with branches intertwined."
Heaven is ancient. The world is old. But, they will die.
This sorrow, like an endless thread, will last forever.

GW

The Song of the Lute, with a Preface

In the tenth year of Yuanhe [816], I was demoted and sent out from the
Capital to Jiujiang as Assistant Prefect there. The following year, in the fall, I
was seeing a friend off at Fenzhou one evening, when I heard a lute-player on
one of the boats. Listening to her music, there was in the way she strummed
her lute a subtle flavor of the Capital. I asked about her, and learned she was
originally an entertainer in Changan. As a girl, she had studied the lute with
the two masters Mu and Cao. When she grew up, and her beauty faded, she
had given herself to a merchant as his wife. Hearing that, I called for more
wine and asked her quickly to play a few more tunes. When she finished, she
sat with a sad look on her face. She told me about her happy childhood in
the Capital and about her hard, sad life now, endlessly wandering from place
to place on rivers and lakes. I had already been away from Changan for two
years, passing my life quite pleasantly. That night, moved by her story, I felt
for the first time like someone who had been banished myself. So I wrote this
long poem as a gift for her, in all 616 characters, and gave it the name, "The
Song of the Lute."

At Xunyang, I was seeing off a friend,
red maple leaves and white reeds rustled with the sound of autumn.
I got down from my horse, and joined my guest on his boat;
we raised our cups and began to drink, but without the sound of song
drinking didn't make us happy, so, sadly we made our goodbyes.
The moon was sinking slowly in the stream,
when we heard, from the darkness on the river, the sound of a lute;
I hurried back, and my guest delayed his leaving.

Searching the source of the music, we called out to the player.
The lute stopped, and in a while we got our answer.
Then we moved our boat closer and invited her to join us;
pouring more wine, relighting the lamps, we revived our little party.
We called to her a thousand times; she finally appeared from the
        darkness,
still half-concealing her face behind her lute.
She turned the pegs and tested her strings:
even before she began to play, these sounds moved us.

The strings rang with a low and mournful sound,
as if to share with us all the disappointments of her life.
With lowered eyes and steady hand, she played,
her music emptying her heart of unbounded sorrows.

Lightly brushing, strumming softly, bending and plucking the
        strings,
first the song *Rainbow Dress*, then *Green Waistband*.

The low strings rang out boldly, like a hard rain falling,
and the high strings softly whispered secrets.
Low and high she wove together as she played,
the sound of pearls, large and small, poured into a jade basin,
then orioles singing beneath bright flowers,
then water bubbling from a dark spring and running down
through pebbles.

Then the spring stopped flowing, as if the strings grew mute;
frozen, the flow stopped, all sound dying away.
A different kind of hidden sadness, a dark regret, was born,
in a silence yet more beautiful than the sound had been.
Then, as if a silver vase had burst, water splashed, a geyser,
iron cavalry charged forth, swords and lances clashing.

She ended the tune with one bold stroke across the lute;
the four strings rang out as one, like ripping silk.
Those in the boats to the east and the west were silent,
not a word, as they gazed upon the autumn moon, white in the
    river's heart.
Thoughtful, as the sound faded, she slid her pick between the
    strings,
straightened her dress, and stood, face somber.

Then she told her story: "I was a girl of the Capital;
my family lived below Frog Mound.
At thirteen, I mastered the lute;
my name ranked first in the Imperial Office of Music.
Each piece I played, teachers praised my art,
and my beauty was envied by all the other women.
Rich young men of Wuling competed to give me gifts;
one tune brought so much red silk, I couldn't count the rolls.
I snapped fine hairpins and silver combs just tapping out the
    rhythm,
stained silk gowns the color of blood, wanton, spilling wine.
I lived for the moment, had no thought of the next,
happily savored autumn moons and spring breezes as they passed.
Then, my protector was drafted and my madam died;
evenings went, mornings came, my beauty faded.
My gate was deserted, all traffic stopped;
grown up, I married myself to a merchant,
who cared more for profit than for constancy.
A month ago, he went to Fuliang, to trade in tea.
Since then, I have lain in the river mouth in this empty boat,
tethered to the bright moon and the cold river.

Late at night, I dream of my childhood;
my own weeping wakes me, my makeup spoiled by tears."

Hearing her lute had made me sigh;
hearing her words made me groan.
We were both bereft here at the ends of the earth;
meeting this way, should it matter we were strangers?

And so I spoke: "I left the Capital last year,
banished here to Xunyang, often lying sick in my bed.
Xunyang is just a country town; there are no real musicians here.
The whole year, I haven't heard the sound of flutes or strings.
I live near the Fen River in a low, damp place,
my house surrounded by yellow reeds and rank bamboo.
And there, what do I hear from dawn till dusk?
Cuckoos' blood-filled calls and sad apes crying.
Spring flowers of the morning or evening's autumn moons,
I always watch alone, pouring and drinking and pouring, alone.
Yes, there are songs in the hills and flutes in the villages,
but they are rustic and tuneless; it's painful to listen.
Tonight, when I heard your lute speak,
it was like the music of the spirits, my ears felt pure again.
So, our stories finished, please sit and play us one more tune,
while I write down for you this 'Song of the Lute.'"

Moved by what I had told her, she stood quietly for a while,
then she sat again and tuned, and played again.
This time the rhythm quickened, yet the song was sadder than
    before;
when she'd finished, all the guests were weeping, faces hidden in
    their hands.
Of those present, who wept most?
Bai Juyi, Assistant Prefect of Jiujiang, his blue gown soaked
    with tears.

GW

Li Shangyin

Han Yu's Memorial Stele

The Emperor of the Yuanhe era was martial and heroic,
the very incarnation of the Yellow Emperor or Fu Xi.
He swore to avenge all insults to his house,
and all nations brought him tribute in the Hall of Justice.
Bandits had ruled west of the Huai for fifty years,
where wolves begat lynxes and lynxes sired bears.
They held the mountains and rivers, and they spread into the plains,
their long lances and sharp spears challenging even the Sun.
The Emperor found a wise minister; his name was Pei Du.
When the rebels tried to kill him, by a miracle, he survived.
Prime Minister's seals at his waist, he was made Campaign
    Commander;
on a dark day, in a cold wind, he raised the Emperor's banner.
His four great generals became his teeth and claws;
a young man from the Ministry of Rites became his adjutant,
an adjutant who was both wise and brave.
His troops were panthers, 140,000 strong.
They attacked Caizhou, dragged the rebels to the Ancestral Temple
    in chains;
the success was incomparable, the Imperial gratitude immeasurable.
The Emperor said, "Du, you are first in achievement;
your Adjutant, Han Yu, should write an inscription in your honor."
Yu bowed his head to the floor, then rose with dancing hands and
    feet,
saying, "I have some talent at inscriptions on metal and stone.
Since antiquity, tasks like this were entrusted to greater writers,
and although it is outside the scope of my official duties,
it has always been said, 'Do not defer doing what is right.'"
When he finished, the Emperor nodded his approval.
Yu withdrew to purify himself, then sitting in a small pavilion
he drenched his great brush in ink.
He chose and emended phrases from the *Canon of Yao* and the
    Canon of Shun,

and drew words from the "Qing Miao" and the "Sheng Min Odes."
At last this marvelous work was done and written on fine paper;
the next morning, paying his respects, he laid it on the crimson steps.
He submitted it saying, "I, your servant, not fearing death,
have recorded these great accomplishments to be carved on a stele."
The stele was thirty feet tall, each character as big as a bushel.
His words were mounted on a sacred tortoise, and decorated with
    dragons.
The language was lofty, the words obscure; few understood it.
He was slandered to the Emperor. They said he concealed some
    censure in these words.
A hundred-foot rope pulled the grand stele down;
with coarse sand and great stones, they ground away his words.

Yet his marvelous writing was like the Primeval Breath,
it had already entered into the hearts and minds of all the people.
Shang Tang's Basin and Confucius' Tripod bore such inscriptions;
the objects themselves are lost, but the words survived.
Alas, past wise Emperors and wise ministers,
had their accomplishments commemorated so they shine brightly
    even now.
But if you won't display Han Yu's marvelous writing to coming ages,
how will you be a match for the Three Sages or the Five Wise Kings?
I wish I could write ten thousand copies, or chant it ten thousand
    times,
until my mouth ran with drool and my right hand was gnarled and
    callused.
I would transmit it onward for seventy-two generations,
to a King who would carve it on jade as the foundation of his
    Audience Hall.

GW

Gao Shi

Song of Yan

In the 26th year of the reign of Emperor Xuanzong, I had a guest from the frontier who recited the "Song of Yan." Moved by these events, I composed this song to match:

Our northeast homes reduced to smoke and dust,
forced to leave our ruined houses,
each man marched off to war with dignity,
encouraged by a blessing from our Emperor.
We crossed Elm Pass to the beat of iron drums,
winding through rocks, flags and banners flying.
Our General gave an urgent order: fly the great desert,
to where the Xiongnu fires blazed beneath Wolf Mountain.

At this distant frontier, all was desolation;
we charged on recklessly through wind and rain.
When half of both our armies had been slaughtered,
inside their tents, the womenfolk still danced and sang.
At autumn's end, the grass was strewn with severed limbs,
the Great Wall abandoned in the setting sun, few men left.
Survivors were treated well, but the last enemy would not give up;
between exhaustion and the mountains, the war proved hard to end.
Armor, so long worn, so tight, took a heavy toll;
complaining muscles failed; they might never heal again.

Back in the city, our young wives were grieving,
while soldiers in the North looked towards home in vain.
With the border winds raging at their most extreme,

how much more desolation could be borne?
When the winds died for a few hours, dense cloud arrived;
we heard the chilling nightly beat of copper drums.
Swords drawn, we looked at one another;
were we prepared to spill our blood and die for honor?

Sir, I present to you the agonies of warfare,
and urge you to remember General Li.

MEF

Li Qi

An Old Soldier's Ballad

In bright sun, we climbed the peaks to look for signal fires;
at dusk, we watered our horses by the rivers of Jiaohe.
In our camps, the sounding watch was muffled by winds thick
    with sand,
yet we heard the sound of a lady's lute, suffused with bitterness.

Under clouds, in desolate places miles beyond our walls,
snow fell and blotted out the endless desert.
Tartar geese cried sadly flying southward, night after night;
hearing them, even Tartar faces ran with tears.

Now, they say the Jade Gate Pass is once more under siege,
so our soldiers risk their lives again, advancing with a light chariots
    force.
Year after year, our dead pile up beyond these wastes,
for nothing more than a few grapevines sent home to the gardens
    of the House of Han.

GW

Wang Wei

Ballad of a Luoyang Girl

The Luoyang girl lives across my lane;
her beautiful face looks barely fifteen.
Her husband's dappled horse has a jade bridle;
maids bring her morsels of carp on golden plates.

Her painted hall looks out on a crimson tower;
red peaches and green willows hang beside the eaves.
Behind thin blinds, she leaves in a carriage of seven fragrant woods;
precious fans welcome her back to nine-flowered bed-curtains.

Her husband is rich, but young and frivolous;
his pride and extravagance surpass even Shi Chong.
He dotes on his mistress, teaches her to dance,
but doesn't hesitate to give gifts of coral to others.

Not till dawn enters spring windows is the ninefold lamp blown out;
from each wick, the embers fly like flowers.
Absorbed in pleasure, she has no time for singing;
her make-up perfect, she sits quietly amid clouds of perfume.

In the town, their friends are all the elegant and refined;
day and night, they socialize among the smartest families.
Who notices or pities the young and lovely girl from Yue,
from a poor family, washing silk at the riverside?

GW

Ballad of an Old General

When he was only fifteen or twenty,
he captured a Tartar cavalry horse to ride.
On South Mountain, he killed a tiger with a white forehead.
In battle, he was the equal of yellow-bearded Cao Zhang.
He fought single-handed across three thousand miles;
with his one sword, he was a match for a million of the enemy.
His army struck quickly, like a thunderclap.
The barbarian horsemen scattered before his chariot spikes.
Wei Qing never lost; Heaven brought him fortune.
Li Guang ended as a failure when his luck ran out.

Since he was dismissed, age has found him
bitter and disappointed as his hair turns white.
In his prime, he could hit a bird in flight;
now, his elbow withered, he cannot draw a bow.
He lives like Zhao Ping, selling melons along the road,
or like Tao Yuanming, planting willows by his gate.
Along his quiet lane, are only failing trees,
from his window, a few cold empty hills.
He swears he would be another Geng Gong, who found water at
    Shule,
not like Guan Fu, his career ruined by drink at Yingchuan.

Armies are gathering beneath the mountains of Helan;
couriers with urgent orders ride day and night.
In the heartland, all the young men are drafted;
the Emperor sends out armies in five directions.
The old General brushes his armor, it shines like snow;
he raises his sword, the engraved stars flashing.
With a bow from Yan, he could kill their Generals.
He feels shame that the enemy has crossed our borders.
Don't ridicule this old Governor of Yunzhong:
he has courage enough for one more battle.

GW

A Ballad of Peach-Blossom Spring

The fisherman paddled up the stream. He loved spring in the
    mountains;
peach blossoms along the bank clustered by the ancient ford.
Watching the scarlet trees he lost track of the miles,
till the stream seemed to end in a place where no one lived.

He passed through a narrow gap in the mountains, a dark and
    twisted way.
Then the mountains opened out onto a broad flat plain.
Far off, he glimpsed something hidden among the clouds and trees.
Coming closer, he saw a thousand homes amid flowers and
    bamboo.
The first he met, he gave his own name in the language of the Han,
but all the village folk were still clothed in the style of the Qin.

Dwelling together here by their magical spring,
they had created a world of their own.
At night, the moon shone down through pines on their quiet homes;
when the sun rose through the clouds, chickens crowed and dogs
    barked.

Excited by a visitor from beyond their world, they gathered around
    him,
hoping to bring him into their houses, to inquire about their
    former home.
At first light, every lane and alley was swept clean of even fallen
    flowers;
At dusk, woodcutters and fishermen floated home on the stream.

In the beginning, in flight from chaos, they had left the world of
    other men.
Later, they lived on like the immortals, never returning.
In their hidden valley, they forgot the world they had left.
Looking in, all one saw were distant hills wreathed in clouds.

Not suspecting how rare it was to find such a place,
worldly cares turned the thoughts of his heart homeward,
so he left the gorge, little marking the hills and rivers he passed.
Then one day he left his family to make the long trip back once more,
saying to himself that his old route could not be confused.
How could he know that those peaks and valleys had changed
     since then?

From the earlier time, all he remembered was going into dark
     mountains,
down a green creek that twisted and turned, to a cloudy forest.
Spring is here and peach blossoms float everywhere on the river;
he never found the magical stream, how could he find the village
     again?

GW

Li Bai

The Hard Road to Shu

Damn, how high and dangerous!
The road to Shu is hard,
harder than climbing to the sky!

Can Cong and Yu Fu
were first to find this boundless land;
forty thousand years went by
before folk risked the border pass to settle here.

West, there's Great White Mountain,
with only pathways fit for birds
towards the peak of Mount Emei.
Brave men have died in sudden landslides
on stairs of stone that hook to heaven.
At the topmost peak, six dragons guard the sun;
below, charging waves attack the river's progress.
Even skillful cranes can't fly across,
and monkeys sulk that they're stuck below.

Those winding paths of Green Clay Mountain!
They zigzag through the boulders: nine turns each hundred steps!
Touch Orion, pass by Gemini, gazing up with awe;
clutch your chest, sit down and gasp for breath.

When will the traveler, heading west, turn back?
These cliffs are just too hazardous to climb.
Birds cry mournfully in ancient trees,
males pursued by females flutter through the woods.
And listen to that cuckoo, crying to the moon,
voicing her sorrow at the empty mountain.

The road to Shu is hard,
harder than climbing to the sky.

Bold men's faces pale on hearing of these perils!
Clustered peaks, barely a foot from the sky,
withered pine-trees, upside-down, hanging over cliffs,
flying waterfalls cascade with deafening din.
Boulders roll and thunder into ravines below.
With danger like this, after traveling so far,
why end up here at all?

Sword Tower stands on one of the steepest spots,
if one man guards this path, ten thousand won't break through;
but if the guards are bandits, it's home to wolves and jackals.
In daylight, watch for savage tigers,
at night, avoid the serpents,
with gnashing teeth that dribble blood
and slash like a knife through hemp.

It's fine to dream of the Brocade City,
but better to have stayed at home.

The road to Shu is hard,
harder than climbing to the sky,
but I'll crawl on westward with a heavy sigh.

MEF

Endless Longing (1)

Oh, this never-ending longing
to be in the capital again.

An autumn cricket cries from the gold well rail;
a light frost has tinged with white my bamboo mat.

My only lamp is dim, dim as my fading hopes;
with many sighs, I raise the blind to watch the moon.

She's lovely as a flower, in her distant cloud;
above, the endless blue of heaven,
below, clear water surging restlessly.

With skies so wide, the road so long, my soul despairs;
my dreaming spirit failed to cross the mountain pass.

This never-ending longing
crushes me inside.

MEF

Endless Longing (2)

After sunset, flowers are wreathed in mist;
a pale moon appears; heartache puts an end to sleep.

A Zhao zither, silent now, rests in its phoenix case;
a Shu lute begins to sound its mandarin duck strings.
There's meaning in the melody no words can impart;
if only spring winds could carry it to Yanran mountain.

Separated by the blue sky, you haunt my memory;
eyes that once looked down so shyly
now brim with tears.

If by any chance you doubt the sorrow in my heart,
come back and see this image in my mirror.

MEF

Hard Road (1)

In my golden cup, pure wine worth ten thousand a pint;
on a jade plate, fine food worth ten thousand coins.
I stop drinking and put down my chopsticks, unable to eat,
draw my sword to dance, look anxiously in all directions.
I want to cross the Yellow River, but ice blocks my way;
I want to climb Mount Taihang, but snow fills the sky.
In idleness I drop a hook into the azure creek,
suddenly, I'm back in my boat, dreaming of distant places.

Traveling is hard!
Traveling is hard!
So many forks in the road—
which one to take?
A great enterprise must find the right moment;
I hoist my sail into the clouds and cross the mighty ocean.

GW

Hard Road (2)

The road is wide,
wide as the blue sky,
but I haven't followed it.
I'd be ashamed to mix with city folk
gambling on cocks and dogs for pears and nuts.

Toying with my sword
I compose a song of bitterness:
to drag my clothes to a prince's door to sell has no appeal.
Out there in the market place, they scoffed at General Han,
and Minister Jia of old was forced to quit.

111

Look here,
in the ancient state of Yan, the King
would humbly sweep the floor for visitors;
with this, he won the loyalty of Ju and Yue,
who gave their hearts and guts to serve him well.
The King's remains are overgrown with creepers;
who now will sweep the floors of Golden Terrace?

The road is hard:
which way to go?

MEF

Hard Road (3)

Got ears? No need to wash them in the Yingshui waters.
Got a mouth? No need to eat the Shouyang ferns.
In this chaotic world, you'd best stay humble;
why rate yourself up there with clouds and moon?

Consider those great sages of the past—
they didn't choose to leave the sunlight,
but brilliance couldn't save them from a sticky end.

There was Zi Xu of Wu, consigned to the River Yu,
Qu Yuan ending it all by the waters of Xiang.
Lu Ji put to death, regardless of his talents,
wishing the execution horn was the cry of Huating cranes.
Li Si, facing his end, regretted not retiring
to his Shangcai home, a falcon on his shoulder.

Then consider Zhang Han of Wu,
enticed by Jiandong autumn winds;
he simply walked away from office.

Enjoy a cup of wine while you're still alive;
dead, what use is a thousand years of fame?

MEF

Please Bring Wine!

Have you not seen, gentlemen,
how the water of the Yellow River rolls down from Heaven,
and flows quickly to the sea without turning back?

Have you not seen, gentlemen,
your elders in the high hall, looking sadly at their hair in the
    mirror,
in the morning like black silk, by evening turned to snow?
At a happy time like this, we must enjoy ourselves;
don't let the golden cups stay empty in this moonlight.

Heaven gave me a talent that I cannot waste;
if I spend my gold on wine, I can get more later.
So, roast the lamb and kill the ox, we'll be happy for a while,
and we'll drink wine, three hundred cups or so.

Master Cen,
friend Dan Qiu,
bring on the wine!
Good Sirs, don't stop,
I will sing a song for you,
so please turn an ear to me and listen.
"Fine music, rich dishes, mean nothing to me,
if I can stay drunk as long as I want, and never be sober.
Since ancient times, sages have lived in obscurity;
only great drinkers have made great names.

"In the old days, the King of Chen gave banquets in his Palace of
    Peace and Joy,
with wine worth a thousand a bottle, their pleasure knew no
    bounds."
Why does our host say that money's run short?
We must buy more, and keep drinking.

My five-colored horse,
my fur coat worth a thousand,
call the boy to take them out to trade for wine:
we'll dissolve the sorrows of ten thousand ages.

G W

Du Fu

Ballad of the Army Carts

Wagons rattling and banging,
horses neighing and snorting,
conscripts marching, each with bow and arrows at his hip,
fathers and mothers, wives and children, running to see them
    off—
so much dust kicked up you can't see Xianyang Bridge!
And the families pulling at their clothes, stamping feet in anger,
blocking the way and weeping—
ah, the sound of their wailing rises straight up to assault heaven.
And a passerby asks, "What's going on?"
The soldier says simply, "This happens all the time.
From age fifteen some are sent to guard the north,
and even at forty some work the army farms in the west.
When they leave home, the village headman has to wrap their
    turbans for them;
when they come back, white-haired, they're still guarding the
    frontier.
The frontier posts run with blood enough to fill an ocean,
and the war-loving Emperor's dreams of conquest have still not
    ended.
Hasn't he heard that in Han, east of the mountains,
there are two hundred prefectures, thousands and thousands of
    villages,
growing nothing but thorns?
And even where there is a sturdy wife to handle hoe and plough,
the poor crops grow raggedly in haphazard fields.
It's even worse for the men of Qin; they're such good fighters
they're driven from battle to battle like dogs or chickens.
Even though you were kind enough to ask, good sir,
perhaps I shouldn't express such resentment.
But take this winter, for instance,
they still haven't demobilized the troops of Guanxi,

and the tax collectors are pressing everyone for land-fees–
land-fees!–from where is that money supposed to come?
Truly, it is an evil thing to bear a son these days,
it is much better to have daughters;
at least you can marry a daughter to the neighbor,
but a son is born only to die, his body lost in the wild grass.
Has my lord seen the shores of the Koko Nor?
The white bones lie there in drifts, uncollected.
New ghosts complain and old ghosts weep,
under the lowering sky their voices cry out in the rain."

DL

A Ballad of Lovely Women

Third day, third month festival, and the air fresh with spring;
beside Serpentine Lake in Changan, many lovely women stroll.
Their appearance is elegant, their thoughts lofty and refined,
their complexions delicate, figures in perfect proportion.
Their embroidered silk gowns glisten with spring light;
golden peacocks and beasts of silver strut upon the fabric.
What is it that they wear upon their heads?
Jeweled headbands with kingfisher feathers, dangling to their
    hairlines.
And what is it that we see upon their backs?
Pearl-studded overskirts drawn tight at the waist.
Among them are kin of the Pepper-flower Chamber with its cloud-
    patterned curtains—
the Duchesses of Guo and Qin, honored with the names of
    nations!
A great roast of purple camel hump rises from a green cauldron,
and crystal plates gleam with heaps of white-scaled fish.
But the rhinoceros horn chopsticks, long-sated, are slow to
    descend,
and the belled knife-handles dance vainly above the roast.
The flying steeds of the eunuchs hardly stir the dust,
as they bear in eight exotic dishes from the Imperial Kitchens.

Then wailing flutes and pounding drums, sad enough to move
    gods or demons,
and a throng of fawning courtiers appears; truly, this is the path of
    power!
The saddle-horse is trailing after; how casually it advances!
Finally, before the balustrade, he dismounts, steps onto patterned
    carpet;
willow-down falls like snow, blanketing white water-weed;
a bluebird takes wing, in its beak a red handkerchief.
You could warm your hands at his power with no need of fire!
Beware of pressing too close, his angry glance may be fatal.

DL

Beside Serpentine Lake

The old man from Shaoling
chokes back his sobs,
wandering the bends of Serpentine
furtively on a spring day:

The riverside palaces
have locked their thousand doors;
for whom do the weeping willows
send forth their new green shoots?
I remember the Emperor's banner
like a rainbow over the Lotus Pool Garden,
and everything in the park
aflame with new color.
The First lady of Zhaoyang palace
rode beside the Emperor in his carriage.
Maids of honor riding before
carried bows and arrows;
their white horses champed at golden bridles
as they bent back their bodies
and loosed arrows at the clouds.
The lady laughed in delight

as one brought down a pair of wings.
The bright eyes, the gleaming teeth,
where are they now? Tainted with blood,
her wandering soul cannot return.
The Wei River flows eastward,
and Jiange Pass is far away.
He who left and she who stayed
can no longer exchange news.
It is only human to have feelings
and soak our bosoms with tears,
but the river's water and its flowers
never change and never care.
In the twilight the city is filled
with the dust of barbarian horsemen.
I want to go to the South City,
but my gaze keeps straying north.

DL

The Pitiful Young Prince

Hooded crows fly at night over the walls of Changan,
uttering harsh cries above Welcoming Autumn Gate,
then head for people's houses, pecking at the lofty roofs,
roofs beneath which high officials scurry to escape barbarians.
The golden whip is broken in two, the nine horses are run to death,
but it is still not possible for all of royal blood to flee together . . .
Wearing in plain sight at his waist precious pendants of jade and
    coral,
the pitiful prince stands weeping at the corner of the road.
When I ask, he refuses to tell either name or surname;
he only speaks of his desperation, and begs to become my slave.
For a hundred days now he has lain hidden in brambles;
there is no whole skin left on his entire body.
But the sons and grandsons of Gaozu all have the same noses—
the dragon-seed, naturally, differs from that of ordinary men.
"Jackals and wolves rule the city, the dragons hide in the wilds;
the prince had better take care of that thousand-tael body!
I don't dare talk long here in plain view by the crossroads,
but for the sake of my prince I will stay for a moment.
Last night the east wind blew in the stench of blood,
and camels from the east filled the former Capital.
The Shuofang veterans were known as skilled warriors,
they always seemed so fierce, but now how foolish they look!
It is rumored that the Son of Heaven has already abdicated,
but also that the Uighur Khan has vowed his loyalty,
that his men gashed their faces and begged to wipe out this disgrace.
Say nothing! Someone else may be hiding and listening.
Alas, Prince, you must be careful, stay on guard,
and may the spirits of the Five Tombs watch over you always."

DL

五言律詩
Five-Word Regulated Verse

Tan Xuanzong

Passing through Zou Lu, Sighing as I Pay Homage to Confucius

So, Confucius, what did you achieve after all,
running around and wearing yourself out in those ancient days?
Your land is now the Zou clan's home.
Your house was razed, rebuilt as a Prince's palace.
You lamented no phoenix appeared in your time, a time of
    troubles.
You grieved when they caught the unicorn, your Way declining.
Now, look at you: we toast you between two great pillars,
something you could only dream of in those bygone days.

GW

Zhang Jiuling

Looking at the Moon; Thinking of Someone Far Away

The moon appears above the ocean:
a moment for all those, worlds apart, to share.
Lovers complain that the night must end;
their passions grow through the long night hours.
I douse the candle with its pitiful light;
and throw on my robe, sensing heavy dew.
Unable to bear to send the gift I hold for you,
I return to sleep and dream of better times.

MEF

Wang Bo

Seeing Off District Defender Du to His Post in Shuzhou

Changan's walls protect the Three Qin lands.
Through the wind and smoke, I can't see the Five Fords.
These thoughts as I part from you,
both of us off again as our duty takes us:
in the whole world there is just you, my friend;
no matter how far you go, we will be like neighbors.
So don't stand here at this fork in our road,
crying like a child, tears soaking your clothes.

GW

Luo Binwang

Imprisoned: Listening to Cicadas

To the west of the palace where I am imprisoned, across the wall, is the courtyard of the Law Section. It has some old scholar trees, like the old trees mentioned by Yin Zhongwen. But the judge here has some sweet crabapple trees like those of Zhao Po. Every evening, when the light of the setting sun reaches the shade under their branches, the cicadas begin to sing. Their faint song brings sad thoughts to those who hear it...

Autumn has come and the cicadas start calling.
A guest here, in my convict's cap, I think even more of home.
How can I endure the way these dark cicadas
come to sing to this white-haired old man?
Because the dew is heavy on their wings, they can't fly close;
in strong winds, their sound is easily lost.
If no one understands how pure these voices are,
who will ever understand what my heart holds?

GW

Du Shenyan

In Reply to Assistant Lu on Jinling's Poem About Early Spring Travels

Only we officials, always traveling,
can be amazed like this at life's renewal.
Pink clouds and white, rising from the sea;
plum blossoms and peach beside the spring river.
Warming air quickens yellow orioles;
new light warms green duckweed.
Then, I hear again an old, old song,
and, thinking of home, I dry a few tears.

GW

Shen Quanqi

Impromptu Poem

I've heard it said, when they garrisoned Yellow Dragon City,
that for years on end they never stood down the troops.
So sad to think the moon that lit their wives' bedrooms
still shines down on their husbands in their camps.
Spring comes and their wives' sadness grows;
at night, men too think of their wives at home.
What general among us can pick up drums and banners
and take that Dragon City so this war can end?

GW

Song Zhiwen

Inscribed at a Staging Post to the North of Dayu Mountains

In the tenth month, geese fly south again;
I'm told it's here they begin their journey back.
As for me, I'm not yet free to leave,
and can't say when that time will come.
The river here is quiet, the tide's about to turn;
heavy vapors still obscure the woods.
Early tomorrow, I'll gaze towards my home.
Who knows? I may see the Gansu plum trees.

MEF

Wang Wan

Beneath Beigu Mountain

The road we travel passes by this blue mountain;
boats float by on the green water before us.
At high tide, the shores are far apart;
the wind freshens and a sail is spread.
The sun rises over the sea in the end of night;
spring on the river is like last year.
Letters home, how can I send them?
Only with the geese returning to Luoyang.

GW

Chang Jian

At a Buddhist College Behind the Temple at Humpback Mountain

On a clear morning, I arrive at the old temple;
the sun's first rays light the high treetops.
A crooked path through dark places
leads to the monks' hall, deep in flowering trees.
This mountain view delights the birds;
the creek-side scene empties my heart.
All sounds of life are stilled here,
save for the chiming of the temple bell.

G W

Cen Shen

Sent to Left Reminder Du Fu

As one, we climb the cinnabar steps,
then each goes off to his office cubicle.
At dawn, we all file in behind the Imperial Regalia;
at dusk, we carry home the odor of the palace.
White-haired, we grieve for fallen blossoms;
from these dark clouds, we envy soaring birds.
Since Imperial decisions are without fault,
our critical petitions will be rather few.

M E F

Li Bai

Presented to Meng Haoran

I love Master Meng,
whose fame has traveled everywhere beneath heaven.
In fresh-faced youth he gave up the official cap and carriage;
white-haired, he rests amid pines and clouds.
Drunk beneath the moon, he often attains sagehood;
dazzled by flowers, he wishes to serve no lord.
How can I aspire to climb such a high mountain?
Humbly I bow to his pure spirit.

DL

Farewell to a Friend at Jingmen Ferry

Traveling far beyond Jingmen ferry,
you'll reach the ancient land of Chu.
Mountains will end in sweeping plains;
the river will flow through vast wastelands.
Beneath the moon, a mirror in the sky,
clouds will carve out ocean mansions.
Sadly, the rivers of our homeland
must bear your boat ten thousand *li*.

MEF

Goodbye to a Friend

Blue mountains spread beyond the north wall,
white water curves east of the city.
This is where we must take our leave:
tumbleweed drifting ten thousand miles.
You'll be companion to the floating clouds,
feel the sunset warmth of old friends.

We wave, you begin to move away;
xiao xiao complain the horses as you go.

MEF

Listening to a Monk of Shu Play His Lute

The monk of Shu, with his lute Green Damask in his arms,
came down the west slope of Mount Emei.
He waved his hands across the strings
like the rustle of pines in ten thousand valleys.
The traveler's mind was refreshed as if by flowing water;
faint echoes tinkled in the frost-ringing bells.
I never noticed the green mountain evening,
nor the dark autumn clouds massing above.

DL

Moored at Night by Cow Island and Thinking of Antiquity

At Cow Island, moored for the night on the West River,
the sky is black, without a single cloud.
I board my boat and look at the autumn moon,
and in that moment, remember General Xie.
Though I have poems I could chant,
he cannot hear me now.
Tomorrow morning, I will spread my sails,
in my wake, maple leaves falling without end.

GW

Du Fu

Moonlit Night

Tonight my wife must watch alone
the full moon over Fuzhou;
I think sadly of my children far away, too young
to understand my absence or remember Changan.
In fragrant mist, her flowing hair is damp;
in clear moonlight, her jade-white arms are cold.
When will we lean at the open casement together,
while the moonlight dries our shining tears?

DL

Regarding This Spring

The nation is torn apart, but mountains and rivers remain;
it's spring in the city, grass and trees grow thick.
Feeling the times, flowers drip with tears;
seeing us parted, birds shriek heart-rending cries.
Soldiers' beacons have burned three months in a row;
I'd give ten thousand in gold for a letter from home.
I scratch my white hair shorter yet—
soon it will be too thin to hold a hatpin.

DL

Spring Vigil at the Imperial Chancery

Shy flowers shelter by the wall at dusk;
birds chatter, flying home to roost.
Stars appear; ten thousand doorways open;
the moon climbs to its zenith in the sky.
Sleepless, I listen for the clash of keys,
imagine every wind-sound is the clink of jade.

Tomorrow's my petition with the Emperor;
time after time, I ask the night: how long?

MEF

In the year 757, I Left the Capital Through the Golden Light Gate and Went by Side Roads to the Court in Exile at Fengxiang. In the Next Year, I Was Sent From My Post as a Left Reminder to a Minor Office in Huazhou. After Bidding Farewell to Some Old Friends, I Left Again Through the Same Gate and Thought Sadly of the Earlier Time

Back then, my duties took me through this gate,
when the country to the west was thick with Tartars.
Even now, my courage has not returned;
I fear my soul has been left behind.
The court is now returning to the Capital;
why have I been sent on this assignment?
I have no talent and every day grow older;
I halt my horse for one last look at the Palace.

GW

Thinking of My Brothers on a Moonlit Night

Warning drums cut off travel this autumn;
over the borderlands a single wild goose calls.
White dew tonight, and the moon
is bright as it was above my old home town.
I have younger brothers, all parted and scattered,
and no family left to ask if they are alive or dead.
I send letters but receive no answers;
how much longer will it be with this war dragging on and on?

DL

Missing Li Bai at the End of the Earth

A cold wind comes up, here at the end of the earth,
and I wonder what your intentions are—
when will my wild goose arrive at last?
Lakes and rivers are swollen this autumn.
Literature hates the writer who does too well;
mountain goblins eagerly await the traveler.
You ought to talk with the wronged ghost of Qu Yuan,
drop him a poem-offering into the Miluo River.

DL

A Second Farewell to Governor Yan Wu at Fengji Post Station

We have come far together, but here we must part;
the green hills echo my feelings in vain.
When will we again take wine cups in hand
to stroll as we did beneath last night's moon?
Every district sings sad songs at your leaving;
three reigns now you have served with distinction.
Now I must go back to my river village alone,
and alone live out the rest of my days.

DL

At the Grave of Grand Marshal Fang

Once again on my way to another district,
I halt my horse at your lonely grave to say farewell.
Recent tears have left no dry soil,
the low sky still heavy with broken clouds.
I used to sit at the go-board with Grand Tutor Xie;
now I am Ji Zha holding his sword above the Xu Lord's grave.
Nothing to see now but the blossoms falling in the wood,
nothing to hear but the oriole's song lingering in my ear as I leave.

DL

Written While Traveling at Night

Sparse grass, a faint wind along the shore,
the tall mast of my solitary boat in the night,
stars hanging low over the flat, wide plains,
moon bobbing up from the great river's waves...
how can a man make a name by writing?
Old age and illness have ended my career.
Drifting, drifting...what am I like?
Between heaven and earth, a wind-blown gull.

DL

On Yueyang Tower

Long ago I heard about the waters of Dongting;
at last I have climbed Yueyang Tower to view them.
Wu and Chu, east and west, are split by the lake;
heaven and earth, day and night, float in its waters.
From friends and relatives, not a word of news.
Old and ill, I have nothing but my little boat.
War horses fill the passes to the north.
I lean on the guardrail, sobbing and weeping.

DL

Wang Wei

At Felloe Creek, Living at Leisure, Presented to Cultivated Talent Pei Di

The cold mountain turns a darker green;
the autumn river murmurs as it always does.
I lean on a staff outside my brushwood gate,
and listen to evening cicadas in a brief breeze.
The setting sun lights the ferry dock;
a wisp of smoke rises above the quiet village.
Then, there you are again, drunk like Jie Yu,
madly singing in front of Five Willows' gate.

GW

Staying in the Mountains on an Autumn Night

Mountains empty after a fresh rain,
at nightfall, the weather feels like autumn.
A bright moon shines through pines;
A clear spring flows over rocks.
Bamboos echo as women return from washing;
lotus move as boats come home from fishing.
Spring grasses always wither when autumn comes.
Will you be staying longer, my fine young friend?

GW

Returning Home to Mount Song

By the clear stream, a narrow pathway:
my horse and carriage follow it at leisure.
The water seems to flow along with me;
birds and I are returning home together.
A ruined wall near an ancient ferry stage;

autumn sunset floods the hills.
Far ahead, beneath Mount Song, my home;
arriving at last, I shall close my door.

Mount Zhongnan

A looming presence near the capital,
cascades of mountains link it to the coast.
Looking back, white clouds are closing in;
before me, nothing to see but heavy mist.
The prospect changes near the central peak:
each valley freshly patterns light and shade.
To sleep overnight in a stranger's home,
I call to the woodsman over the river.

Reply to Vice-Prefect Zhang

These last few years, I search for quietude;
worldly concerns no longer trouble me.
I've made myself no long-term strategy,
but instinct guides me back to these old woods.
I ease my belt in fresh pine breezes,
play my lute to the mountain moon.
You question me on failure or success?
The song of a fisherman drifts across the bay.

Visiting Fragrance Accumulated Temple

I didn't know about Fragrance Accumulated Temple,
miles up among cloud-wrapped peaks.
Walking a deserted path through ancient trees,
where was the bell I heard deep in the mountains?

A spring gurgled, choked by huge rocks,
and pale sunlight chilled green pines.
In dim twilight beside a quiet pool,
meditation conquers the mind's poison dragons.

DL

Farewell to Prefect Li, Who Leaves to Take Up His Post at Zizhou

In ten thousand ravines, ancient trees touch the sky;
a thousand mountains fill with sad cuckoos calling.
After a night of rain in those mountains,
water pours from the branches like a hundred streams.
Han women will pay their taxes in tong cloth;
Ba men will sue each other over taro fields.
The Old Literary Gentleman transformed them in his day;
build on his old achievements to make yours new.

GW

About to Set Sail on the Han River

At Chu's border, where the three branches of the Xiang River join.
When you pass Jingmen, the nine streams flow as one.
The great river rolls onward, to the end of the world,
as mountains on either side fade in and out of view.
Towns along the banks float above the water;
waves seem to move against some far-off sky.
Such a beautiful day here in Xianyang,
I wish I could stay longer to drink with Old Man Shan.

GW

South Mountain Retreat

In my middle years, I embraced the Way
and lately made my home near South Mountain,
to wander at will through the countryside, alone,

empty of purpose, but making new discoveries.
I walk out to where a stream begins,
sit and watch the clouds drift overhead.
If, by chance, I meet an old woodsman,
we'll talk and laugh, no thought of going home.

MEF

Meng Haoran

A View of Lake Dongting, for Minister Zhang Jiuling

In the eighth month, the lake is at its fullest;
reflected sky and water, joined in endless blue.
Its breath rises like steam from the Yunmeng marshes,
its waves roll across to shake the Yueyang city wall.
I would cross the lake, but have no boat or oars;
I'm ashamed to be idle in such enlightened times.
I sit and watch men dangle fishing lines,
envying them in vain for each fish caught.

GW

Climbing Mount Xian with Friends

In the world of men, nothing stays unchanged;
from ancient times until today, there's always flux,
but rivers and mountains never lose their splendor;
like those who came before, we're moved to visit them.
Past rapids, fish in shallows near a bridge,
a cold sky, the depths of Yunmen Swamp,
to the stone monument for the Duke of Yang:
reading the inscription, our sleeves are wet with tears.

MEF

A Feast at the House of Daoist Priest Mei, on Qingming Day

Resting in my woodland home, mourning the end of spring,
I opened the door, looked out on the shining scene.
Suddenly, a bluebird messenger arrived,
inviting me to the house of Red Pine.
Cinnabar was flaming in a crucible;
the Peaches of Immortality were about to bloom.
If we could hold on to that glowing moment,
how we'd cherish the Wine of Rosy Clouds!

MEF

In the Twilight of the Year I Return to the South

I give up petitioning the palace towers in the north;
I return to my poor cottage in the hills of the south.
Saying I had no talent, the Shining Ruler cast me aside.
My illnesses are many, my friends scattered and few.
White hair makes plain my passing years;
green sunniness heralds the coming spring.
Depressed and brooding, I cannot sleep;
the moon shines through pines, but my window is empty.

DL

Visiting an Old Friend's Country Place

My old friend prepared chicken and millet,
and invited me to visit his country place.
Green trees grow thick beside his village;
blue hills slant beyond the city wall.
We open a window to look out on the little square;
with our wine, we chat about mulberries and hemp.
He tells me I should wait until the Double Ninth day,
then come again to enjoy his chrysanthemums.

GW

Autumn Feelings from Qin, Sent to Monk Yuan

I would find a mountainside to settle on,
if only I had a hermit's fortitude.
It's not my wish to stay here in the north,
when the master I revere is in the eastern forests.
As golden cassia, burning, quickly turns to ash;
so my high ideals have crumbled with the years.
Day and night, the winds blow bitter here;
cries of cicadas deepen the desolation.

MEF

Poem Sent to Old Friends While Staying Overnight in Donglu

In these gloomy mountains I hear the sad calls of apes;
like the blue river, night flows in quickly.
Wind cries in the leaves of both riverbanks;
the moon shines down on my solitary boat.
Jiande county is not my home—
I think of old companions in Yangzhou city.
I write out two lines of tears
and send them far downstream to the west.

DL

Farewell to Censor Wang Wei

Alone in the end, why have I been waiting,
returning each morning without purpose?
Now I must go where grass is sweeter;
sadly I must leave my old friend.
On the road, who will help me?
True friends are rare in this world.
Only by embracing solitude,
shall I bear to close at last my humble gate.

GW

Memories, as Cold Arrives Early on the River

Leaves fall, wild geese fly south,
the north wind strikes cold on the river.
My home stands where the Xiang River bends,
as out of reach as the clouds above.
I put an end to homesick tears,
and scan the horizon for a single sail.
Losing my way to the ferry dock, I'll have to ask.
At dusk, a calm and endless sea.

MEF

Liu Changqing

On an Autumn Day, Climbing to the Temple on Duke Wu's Terrace, to Look into the Distance

On the old terrace littered with leaves shaken from the trees,
moody in autumn, I look out toward my old home.
The temple is remote, few people come,
only peaks that loom in clouds across the deep river.
As the last light of evening lingers on the ruined fortress,
the ringing of a cold stone bell fills the empty forest.
Sad, sad, the stories of those southern kingdoms;
here, now, the Great River flows out of the past alone.

GW

Seeing Off Vice Censor-in-Chief Li on His Way Back to His Home at Hanyang

This rootless wanderer, once the general who pacified the South,
rode at the head of an army of a hundred thousand.
Dismissed from office now, with nothing to go home to,

he is old and exiled, brooding on his lost glories.
When he alone stood up, our borders were all peaceful;
he risked his life where a single blade could end it.
Now, in this vast emptiness, adrift on great rivers,
the sun goes down on his hopes to bring it back.

G W

Farewell to Wang the Eleventh, Traveling South

Through mist across the wide river,
sleeves wet with tears, I watch and wave.
Birds fly off; who knows where?
Ahead, blue mountain desolation.
A distant sail on the Yangzi river;
a spring sunset at Five Lakes.
Who is here to see, on White Apple Island,
a solitary, grieving figure?

M E F

Searching for Dao Master Chang at South Stream

Along the path I find clog-prints in the moss.
White clouds rest upon the tranquil islet.
Fragrant grasses block the idle gate;
after rain, the pines are a deeper green.
Climbing the slope of the mountain,
I reach the source of the stream.
Flowers beside it reveal the Zen idea—
facing them, I also have no need for words.

D L

Written on New Year's Day

Thoughts of home cut deep on New Year's Day,
alone and tearful at the end of the earth.
Grown old before I can leave this place,
spring after spring still finds me here.
Morning and evening, mountain apes my companions;
I share the wind and mist with willows on the shore.
Now, I am like Jia Yi, exiled to Changsha;
how many more years till I go home again?

GW

Qian Qi

To a Buddhist Monk Returning to Japan

Brought to the Supreme Nation by fate,
your path here was like dream travel.
You floated across the broad blue sea to heaven;
now you leave our land, your dharma boat light.
Moon and water understand the stillness of meditation;
fish and dragons attend your Buddhist chants.
I cherish the image of your single lamp—
still bright across ten thousand miles.

DL

Sent to Censor Yang from My Study in Gukou

From this thatched hut, nestling in a river gully,
I view cloudscapes through a screen of climbing figs.
I enjoy bamboo made fresh by rainfall,
and love the view of the mountain range at sunset.
Idle egrets come here, settling quite early;

autumn flowers flourish, linger late.
My houseboy swept the pathway clear of creepers
for you, my friend, expected yesterday.

MEF

Wei Yingwu

On the Huai River, Meeting an Old Friend from Liangzhou

Once, we were traveling between the Yangzi and the Han,
each time we met, we drank together before moving on.
After we parted, we were floating clouds;
ten years passed by, flowing like a river.
Now, we are happy again, as then,
but we are older, our hair is turning gray.
You ask me why I don't head homeward;
I point to the autumn hills above the Huai.

GW

Seeing Off Li Zhou in Evening Rain

Drizzle on the Yangzi river;
a twilight bell from Jianye.
The sail of your boat hangs heavy, soaked with mist;
in this gloomy weather, birds are leaving late.
The river mouth is somewhere out of sight;
all we see are glistening trees at the water's edge.
Overcome by the sadness of farewell,
our sleeves are doubly wet with rain and tears.

MEF

Han Hong

Replying to Cheng Yan's Poem Called "Impromptu on an Autumn Night"

Long bamboos leaned in a breeze;
the empty city lay quiet in the moonlight.
One goose flew across the River of Stars;
from a thousand houses came the clatter of washboards.
The chill foretold the end of autumn;
I slept late, knowing we would meet that night.
All night long we chanted your elegant lines
till dawn surprised us with the cries of crows.

G W

[Title Lost]

The path here ends among white clouds,
in spring, as long as this blue creek.
Now and then, flowers float past,
lending perfume to the flowing water.
My quiet gate faces the mountain road;
my study is deep among willow trees.
Sometimes the sun breaks through this shade,
shining in to brighten my faded robe.

G W

Dai Shulun

Old Friends Meeting by Chance at an Inn

Autumn night, full moon light;
by the city gate, one chance in a thousand:
meeting again, here in the South.
This surely happens only in dreams.
A breeze in the branches wakes the magpies;
dew evicts the insects from the grass.
We travelers drink together through the night,
parting only when the dawn bell sounds.

G W

Lu Lun

Farewell to Li Duan

My old garden is filled with withered grass;
about to leave, I am filled with sadness.
My road leads off beyond cold clouds;
snow falls in the dusk as I take my leave.
I was orphaned young and became a wanderer;
in a life full of hardship, I met you late.
Now, face to face, we can't stop tears;
in a world of turmoil, where will we meet again?

G W

Li Yi

Happy to Meet My Cousin, Only to Hear Him Say Farewell

After ten years, separated by a world at war,
we meet again, and you have become a man.
When I first saw you, I asked who you were;
then your name brought back your face when young.
Since we parted, the whole world has changed;
the evening bell sounds, no more to say.
Tomorrow, you are on the road to Baling,
beyond these mountains, too many to count.

GW

Sikong Shu

Overnight at Yunyang Staging Post; Farewell to Han Shen

Friends from way back, parted in this vast terrain;
how long have hills and rivers stood between us?
To meet like this so suddenly—it's like a dream.
Sadly we ask each other where the years have gone.
My lone lamp's glow reveals cold rain;
swirling mist darkens deep bamboo.
More sorrow lies in wait tomorrow, when
we'll share that final farewell cup.

MEF

Happy That My Cousin Lu Lun Stays the Night

Nights pass in silence; no neighbors hereabout;
poor, I'm obliged to live in this forsaken spot.
Where raindrops scatter over withered leaves,
this white-haired ancient sits beneath his lamp.
So I've stagnated here for all these years,
ashamed you come to visit me so frequently.
Throughout our lives you've always shared with me;
how fortunate for me that we are family!

MEF

Now That the Rebels Are Defeated, Farewell to a Friend Returning Northward

When the world was torn apart, we fled south together;
now there is peace, but only you are returning north.
While my hair turns white in this foreign place,
you will see again the green hills of our old home.
As a dawn moon moves above ruined battlements,
under a million stars, I'll still lodge by this old pass.
Cold birds and withered grass,
everywhere companions to my mournful face.

GW

Liu Yuxi

The Temple of the King of Shu

Heaven and earth were so full of his martial spirit,
that a thousand autumns later, we still respect him.
Though fate split the world into three kingdoms,
in his, the old Han coins were still accepted.
With his able minister, he established his dynasty,
but the son who followed him had not his father's wisdom.
Saddest of all, his son's beloved dancing girls,
ended up performing in the palaces of Wei.

GW

Zhang Ji (1)

To a Friend Lost in the Tibetan War

Last year you were sent to garrison Yuezhi;
soon the whole army was destroyed below the walls.
Now, with the Tibetan border sealed, no news comes;
are you dead, or alive, wandering that distant land forever?
No one was sent to bring back the abandoned tents;
a few horses returned with torn flags we couldn't make out.
I would have a ceremony for you, but what if you are alive?
All I can do is shed tears for you, lost at the end of the sky.

GW

Bai Juyi

A Farewell Poem on the Theme "Grass on the Old Plain"

See how the grass flourishes on this old plain,
each year, once withered, then green again.
Wild fires can't burn it all;
when the spring winds blow, it grows again.
Now, its fragrance overruns the old road,
in clear spring sunlight, green up to the ruined walls.
So here I say farewell to my honored friend,
and the grass rustles, full of parting's sorrows.

GW

Du Mu

Staying at an Inn

Staying at the inn alone, no friends,
no one to share my mournful thoughts.
Under a cold lamp, I think about my life;
the cries of a lost goose wake me from sad sleep.
In my dream, I traveled far, almost home by dawn;
when my family sends letters, they take a year to find me.
Outside on the darkened river, the moon in mist,
still tethered by the gate, a fisherman's boat.

GW

Xu Hun

Autumn Day: Inscribed at Tong Pass Staging Post on My Way to the Capital

Evening comes; red leaves are rustling.
A wine-gourd welcome waits at this Long Pavilion.
Drifting clouds gather over Hua Mountain;
a rain-shower crosses Zhongtiao Peak.
Trees color the furthest mountain ranges;
the river babbles, pursuing a distant ocean.
Tomorrow I'll reach the Capital, dreaming still
of living as a woodsman or a fisherman.

MEF

Early Autumn

The pure sound of a lute fills the long night;
a west wind shakes the blue wisteria.
The last fireflies nest among pearls of dew;
fall's first geese brush the River of Stars.
Tall trees at dawn, still lush with leaves;
far mountains, endless in pure light.
One leaf falls south of the Huai,
and I feel the waves rise on Lake Dongting.

GW

Li Shangyin

Cicada

Hard to be so lofty and sate your hunger;
futile, your whispers of distress.
By the fifth watch, you've faded out,
your green tree host indifferent to your fate.
Scholar, tree-branch, both were helpless in a flood.
My yard's already overgrown with weeds.
I'm troubled, sir, by your warning song:
down here we too survive on empty air.

MEF

Wind and Rain

Saddened by the words of *precious sword*,
I've wandered, squandering the years.
Yellow leaves still suffer wind and rain
as music lures me to the green pavilions;
today's encounters merely fleeting things
unlike the warmth of old companionships.
To ease my heart, I reach for Xinfeng wine;
a thousand gallons wouldn't melt this sorrow.

MEF

Falling Blossoms

Guests have left the high pavilion;
in the little garden, petals fly in chaos.
They fall in patches on the curving path,
drifting far towards the sunset.
Heartbroken, I can't bear to sweep them;
I watch them, and long for their return.
My heart dies at the end of spring;
tears, for sure, will soak my clothes.

GW

Cold Thoughts

You left; waves lap at my doorstep.
Cicadas now sit mute on dew-filled branches.
This is the time of year for memories;
I lean in contemplation for a while.
Spring's distant as the dipper in the north;
no messenger has reached me from the south.
Here, at the world's end, I search for signs in dreams
to ease suspicions that you've found another friend.

MEF

Green Vines North

As the fading sun sets behind the mountains,
I come to visit a solitary monk, his thatched hut.
Fallen leaves on the ground, no sign of him.
Cold clouds shroud the onward path, how many layers?
I imagine him ringing the stone bell once at dusk,
or leaning peacefully against his rattan staff.
The infinite universe is barely a speck of dust,
so after all, what point to my petty loves and hates?

GW

Wen Tingyun

Farewell to a Traveler, Eastward Bound

As yellow leaves are falling at this desolate post,
on impulse, you decide to leave.
A high wind blows at Hanyang ferry crossing,
as the sun rises over Yongmen mountain.
Few of us are left now at the riverside,
as your lone boat heads towards the sky's end.
When will we meet again, I ask,
with cups of wine to ease the pain of separation?

GW

Ma Dai

Lodging on the Ba River in Autumn

Wind and rain linger on the plains of Ba;
at evening, rows of geese fly over.
Leaves fall from the trees in this strange place;
by an old lamp, this man alone in the night.
White dew settles in an empty garden;
across the wall, country monks my neighbors.
Here too long, outside my gate, a wasteland;
what year, I wonder, will I serve my Prince again?

GW

Thoughts of Antiquity on a Chu River

Cold dew settles in evening light;
the faint sun sets behind Chu hills.
In trees by the lake, apes cry;
I drift in my orchid boat.
A bright moon rises over broad marshland;
streams rush in dark valleys.
The Lord in the Clouds does not appear;
all night I am alone in autumn sadness.

GW

Zhang Qiao

Message from the Frontier

The sound of bugles has faded in the clear autumn air;
soldiers lean idly against the battlements on the watchtower.
Spring breezes ruffle the grass on Zhaojun's tomb,
as the sun sets over Liangzhou.
Now, the desert is no longer blocked by fighting;
travelers come and go across these open spaces.
Peace with the Barbarians gathers like the river;
long may it flow towards the south!

GW

Cui Tu

Thoughts at the Road to the Three Ba on New Year's Eve

On the endless road to the Three Ba,
I've come ten thousand perilous miles.
Snow lingers on the mountains, here and there;
spring will find me stranded in this alien place.
The further I am from my flesh and blood,
the more I turn to my servant boy.
With all this aimless drifting, how can I face
tomorrow's beginning of another year?

MEF

A Lone Wild Goose

So many echelons have crossed the border,
how did you end up as their shadow?
Lost in rain at twilight, calling out to them,
too late, you settle on an icy pool.
Crossing to an island to escape looming clouds,
the cold border moon will be your guide.
Here's hoping you'll succeed in flying back alone,
and not fall victim to some hunter's arrow.

MEF

Du Xunhe

Spring Lament in the Palace

Cursed from early days by beauty,
I've grown too indolent to face a mirror.
Beauty alone will not appease the Emperor;
who will school me in beguiling ways?
Birds call and chatter in the warm spring breeze,
overhead, the sun casts blossom shadows.
Each year, I remember the girls back in Yue,
those times we gathered lotus flowers together.

MEF

Wei Zhuang

Night Thoughts of Zhangtai

Through the long night, a zither laments,
strings pulsing with the grief of wind and rain.
A solitary lamp, a distant bugle;
the crescent moon sinks beyond the Zhangtai.
Fragrant grasses are already withering
and still my friend has not arrived.
No way now to send a letter home:
wild geese have gone, and carried autumn south.

MEF

The Monk Jiaoran

Looking for Lu Hongche but Not Finding Him at Home

Although your new place is near the city walls,
the path to reach it goes through mulberry and hemp.
The chrysanthemums you planted by your fence,
though autumn comes, have not yet shown their flowers.
I knocked at your gate, but no dog barked;
so I had to ask your western neighbor.
He told me you had gone into the mountains,
but returned each day under the setting sun.

GW

七言律詩
Seven-Word Regulated Verse

Cui Hao

Yellow Crane Tower

They say a man mounted a yellow crane here and flew away,
leaving behind in this empty place the Yellow Crane Tower.
The yellow crane, once gone, never came back,
only white clouds, silently flowing past for a thousand years.
Across the sunlit river, bright the trees of Hanyang;
fragrant grass, lush and green on Parrot Island.
In the setting sun, I cannot see my old home,
only waves of mist on the river, and sadness comes.

GW

Passing Huayin

The soaring mass of Taihua Mountain towers over Xianyang;
its three peaks beyond the sky, no chisels cut them.
Clouds about to part before the Martial Emperor's temple,
rain just clearing over the Immortal's Palm.
North of the river, hemmed in by the Hangu Pass,
the post road westward leads to the Han Altar.
Those of you hurrying by on the road, striving for fame and
fortune,
would be better off staying here to learn the Way of long life.

GW

Zu Yong

The View from Jimen

Climbing Yan Terrace, I feel pangs of sorrow,
as fifes and drums sound across the old Han encampment.
Ten thousand miles of snow beneath a cold winter sky;
the whole frontier full of battle flags in the light of morning.
In the desert, signal fires stretch out toward the Tartar moon;
far off, by the seashore, clouded peaks surround Jimen.
In my youth, I didn't throw away the brushes of a scribe,
but still I yearned for trophies of success in battle.

GW

Li Qi

Saying Goodbye to Wei Wan, Returning to the Capital

At dawn, the traveler sings his farewell song;
overnight, the first light frost had crossed the river.
Painful, the sound of wild geese overhead,
the view of cloud-topped mountains in the traveler's path.
By closed city gates, trees will soon change color from the cold;
in the Imperial Park at dusk, you'll hear the din of washboards.
I can't say I'm mad about the pleasures of the Capital;
it's where too many wasted years slipped by.

MEF

Cui Shu

On the Double Ninth, Climbing the Immortal's Lookout Terrace, Presented to District Magistrate Liu Rong

The Han Emperor Wen built a tall terrace;
today we climb it to look down on dawn's glory.
To the north lie the Three Jins, among clouded peaks;
to the east lie the Two Tombs, sending wind and rain.
Who now remembers Yin, the Guardian at the Gate,
or the Old Immortal of the River, who vanished through it?
Enough! I will go and look for Tao Yuanming,
together, we'll get drunk on chrysanthemum-sprinkled wine.

GW

Li Bai

Climbing Phoenix Terrace at Jinling

Here on Phoenix Terrace the phoenix once paraded.
Terrace empty, phoenix gone, the river flows on.
Wu palace pathways are peacefully overgrown;
the caps and robes of Jin lie buried under grave-mounds.
Over there, the Three Peaks are dim beyond green hills;
White Eagle Island, here, divides one river into two.
Drifting clouds, as always, are blanketing the sun,
deepening my distress that Changan can't be seen.

MEF

Gao Shi

Farewell to District Defender Li, Demoted to Xiazhong, and District Defender Wang, Demoted to Changsha

My friends, how should we feel about this parting?
Stop your horses to have a drink, tell me where you're going.
One of you will pass through the Wu Gorge in tears, apes calling
    from the banks;
from Hengyang, each homeward goose will bring your letters.
On Green Maple River, autumn sails are far away;
by White Emperor City, old trees are sparse and bare.
In this enlightened age, by our Emperor's grace,
we part only for a while, so no need to delay your steps.

GW

Cen Shen

Early Morning Session at the Shining Palace; Matching Secretary Jia Zhi's Poem

Cock-crow: the palace road in cold dawn light.
An oriole welcomes spring from the palace wall.
Sunrise bell at the Golden Gate; a thousand doors thrown open;
on jade steps, warrior figures greet officials crowding in.
A pattern of swords and pendants; stars begin to fade;
willows brush with flags and banners, damp with dew.
Alone by the Phoenix pool, a guest is singing,
with unmatched artistry, an ancient springtime song.

MEF

Wang Wei

Harmonizing Secretariat Drafter Jia's Poem: "Morning Audience at the Palace of Great Brightness"

The Master of Cock-crow, in his scarlet cap, proclaims the hour of
    dawn;
the Chief Steward for the Wardrobe brings in the kingfisher coat.
Throughout the ninefold palace, every door is opened;
envoys from ten thousand kingdoms bow to his jeweled crown.
Sunlight first strikes the palace doors, decorated with Immortals'
    palms;
perfumed smoke begins to float near the Emperor's dragon robe.
After morning Court, you must draft His edicts on five-colored
    paper,
so, girdle pendants ringing, you rush to the Phoenix Pool.

                                                                    GW

A Poem Written at the Emperor's Command, to Rhyme His Composition Entitled "Enjoying the Spring Scenery While Held Up by a Spring Shower en Route from the Fairyland Palace to the Pavilion of Flourishing Fortune by Way of the Covered Passage"

The Wei River winds its way through the frontier of Qin;
the Yellow Mountain Palace, as in Han times, spreads out along its
    shore.
The Emperor's carriage emerges from the willows of a thousand
    courtyards;
from the covered way, he turns to look at the flowers in his gardens.
Amid the clouds, the Imperial City's twin gate towers;
in the rain, the spring trees of ten thousand houses.
This Imperial Progress suits the Yang breath of the season,
and is not merely to take idle pleasure from a world in flower.

                                                                    GW

After Long Rain, Written at Wanchuan Village

After days of rain, smoke rises late above the woods,
where farmers are steaming greens and millet.
Egrets fly across the misty paddy-fields;
orioles call from treetops under summer clouds.
In the quiet of these hills at dawn, hibiscus is unfolding;
under a pine tree, mallow seeds suffice to break my fast.
This old man no longer vies with others for position,
why then, does this seagull still eye me with suspicion?

MEF

Replying to Supervising Secretary Guo

At your high tower, the last light fades on pairs of gates,
peaches and plums cast shade as willow catkins dance.
In the offices, an evening bell sounds;
in the Chancellery, few work, only birds chatter.
At dawn, jade pendants chiming, you hurry to the Golden Hall;
at dusk, with Imperial Edicts, you leave through the lacquered
    door.
I would like to serve there with you, but old age prevents me;
now I will take to my sickbed, and set aside my official robes.

GW

Du Fu

The Chancellor of Shu

For the Chancellor's shrine, where should one look?
On the outskirts of Chengdu where cypresses grow thick.
On its steps emerald grass gleams, wearing spring only for itself;
screened by leaves a yellow oriole sings, its lovely sound unheard.
Three humble, imploring visits yielded a plan for world order;
two reigns he founded and assisted, showing his faithful heart.
He led the army out against Wei, but died himself before victory;
at the thought of it, brave men will always shed tears.

DL

Welcoming a Guest

Spring floods approach my house from north and south,
now flocks of seagulls visit every day.
My pathway's long unswept for visitors—
but the rustic gate stands open for my guest.
The town's so far away, there's plain food only,
just old and sorry wine left in the jar,
but if you're game to share with my old neighbor,
we'll find an extra cup and call him over.

MEF

Looking at the Countryside

West mountain in white snow, three towns guarded;
southern shore of a clear river, bridges a thousand *li* apart.
The whole country in wind and dust, my brothers scattered;
alone at the end of the world, my tears fall.
Past my prime now, old and sick,
never of service to my country,

161

I'll mount my horse, ride out beyond the city,
unable to endure the bleakness of our lives.

G W

On Learning That Our Troops Have Retaken Henan and Hebei

The soldiers have retaken Hebei! Word has just come through
    Jiange Pass.
As soon as I hear this, my robe is soaked with tears.
I turn to look at my wife and children—where did all our sorrow
    go?
I pack up my poems helter-skelter, so happy I'm witless.
Broad day, and I am singing aloud—it's time for some wine!
With green spring for company, what a joyful trip home!
We'll go straight from Ba Gorge down through Wu Gorge,
then on to Xiangyang and home, home to Luoyang!

DL

Climbing High

Sharp wind, towering sky, apes howling mournfully;
untouched island, white sand, birds flying in circles.
Infinite forest, bleakly shedding leaf after leaf;
inexhaustible river, rolling on wave after wave.
Through a thousand miles of melancholy autumn, I travel;
carrying a hundred years of sickness, I climb this terrace alone.
Hardship and bitter regret have frosted my temples—
and what torments me most? Giving up wine!

DL

Climbing the Tower

Flowers by the high tower hurt the visitor's heart;
troubles are everywhere as I climb up to look down.
Spring colors along Brocade River bring heaven to earth;
floating clouds on Jade-fort Mountain blend then and now.
The court, like the North Star, in the end remained fixed;
may the Tibetans, west in the mountains, cease their raiding.
Even the pathetic Second Ruler still has his temple—
at the end of this day I will make a Liangfu song.

DL

Passing the Night at the General's Headquarters

Clear autumn at headquarters, *wutong* trees cold beside the well;
I spend the night alone in the river city, burning my candle down.
Sad bugle notes sound through the long night as I talk to myself;
glorious moon hanging in mid-sky but who looks?
The endless dust-storm of troubles cuts off news and letters;
the frontier passes are perilous, travel nearly impossible.
I have already suffered ten years, ten years of turmoil and hardship;
now I am forced to accept a perch on this one peaceful branch.

DL

Night in the Pavilion

At the end of the year, Yin and Yang make the days shorter;
at the end of the earth, frost and snow brighten cold nights.
Drums and trumpets, sad and loud, wake me at dawn,
the River of Stars still shining above the Three Gorges.
In the countryside, a thousand families weep at word of war;
everywhere, fishermen and woodcutters sing Tartar songs.
Zhuge Liang and Gongsun Shu both ended up dead in yellow earth;
my days run out here, alone, with no word from home.

GW

Elegies on Ancient Sites (1)

Scattered in north and east beyond wind and dust;
adrift in south and west between heaven and earth.
Lingering endlessly in Three Gorges' towers and terraces;
mingling clouds and mountains with garments of the Five Streams.
The barbarian served his master, but in the end betrayed him;
the poet lamented his times, but could never go home.
Yu Xin's whole life was filled with sadness,
but the poems of his later years moved the world.

GW

Elegies on Ancient Sites (2)

Watching leaves wither and fall, I know Song Yu's sorrow;
in his elegance and erudition I find my teacher.
Thinking of him and a thousand autumns, my tears fall
that the same sadness can be felt in such different ages.
In his old home between river and mountains, only his poems
    remain;
on the abandoned terrace of clouds and rain, was it all a dream?
Sadder still, the Chu palaces were wiped away;
these days, the boatmen cannot show us where they stood.

GW

Elegies on Ancient Sites (3): Birthplace of Wang Zhaojun

Through flocks of mountains, myriad valleys, I arrive in Jingmen,
where Radiant Lady was born and bred—the village is still there.
Once she left the red palace walls, there was nothing but endless
    desert;
only her evergreen grave is left to face the twilight.
A portrait once recorded her spring-fresh face;
the tinkle of girdle pendants heralds her soul's vain return by
    moonlight.

For a thousand years the *pipa* has wailed in its alien tongue,
as if its strings bemoan in song her tragic tale of grief.

DL

Elegies on Ancient Sites (4)

The Lord of Shu coveted Wu, coming down the Three Gorges;
the next year, he died in the Yongan Palace.
On the empty mountains, I can imagine his feathered banners;
in this ruined shrine, I see his glorious palace.
Now, cranes roost in the cypress by his ancient temple,
where only old villagers come for the summer and winter rites.
Zhuge Liang's temple is not far away,
where pilgrims honor King and Minister together.

GW

Elegies on Ancient Sites (5): Zhuge Liang

Zhuge's famous name hangs over the whole world;
the revered statesman's portrait awes with its sublimity.
The empire carved into thirds hindered his designs,
yet he soars through the ages, a lone feather in the sky.
He is brother to such greats as Yi Yin and Lu Shang;
if he had established control, Xiao and Cao would be forgotten.
But the cycle had passed; Han fortunes could not be restored.
His military strategy a failure, his hopes dashed, his body perished.

DL

Liu Changqing

To Officials Xue and Liu, on Leaving Jiangzhou Again

How can I follow the "Excellent Imperial Edict"
when all I learned from the world of men is wine and song?
Wild geese from Tartar lands fly over the moonlit river;
trees tumble south of Huai, leaving mountains bare.
Living contented for a while in a hermit's paradise,
who'd respect an old man with hair turned white?
Now the Imperial Bell has rung for all those growing old;
In shame, my friends, I warn you: watch out for wind and waves.

MEF

At Changsha, Visiting the House Where Jia Yi Lived

You served three years down here in your demotion,
a land still heavy with Qu Yuan's ancient sorrow.
So long after you left, I came here through autumn grass,
through the cold empty forest, in the slanting light of dusk.
Emperor Wen ruled well, yet you he slighted;
as the Xiang rolled by, did it hear your elegy?
Standing in this solitude of silent hills and rivers,
I wonder why you came to such a god-forsaken place at all.

GW

En Route from Xiakou to Parrot Island at Night, a View of Yueyang, Sent to Vice Censor-in-Chief Yuan

By the island, the river is calm and the night sky clear;
traveling here in Chu, my thoughts wander back to the past.
Above Hankou, birds pass by in the last light of dusk;
Lake Dongting in autumn seems to reach the distant sky.
From the remote town, its back to the hills, a bugle in the chill,
as we moor for the night among the lonely soldiers on guard.
I recall Jia Yi wrote earnestly his advice to the Han Court;
mourned by all since, he was banished for his heartfelt words.

GW

Qian Qi

For Imperial Palace Secretary Pei

In the second month, yellow orioles fly in the Imperial Gardens,
spring mornings in the courtyard, still dark before sunrise.
The sound of bells from the Changle Palace fades beyond the
    flowers;
weeping willows by Dragon Pool glisten from the rain.
The sun cannot warm the cold sadness of my failed career;
looking up at stars through the clouds, I still wish I could serve.
Ten years of my petitions have met with no response;
when I glimpse your official hairpin, I'm ashamed of my thin
    white hair.

GW

Wei Yingwu

Sent to Li Dan

We parted last year when the flowers were blooming;
now, they bloom again—it's been a year.
The currents in our lives are so hard to predict;
this spring melancholy stays with me as I fall asleep alone.
I've been sick lately, and think about going home;
my district is full of refugees, I'm ashamed to take my pay.
I heard you were thinking about coming for a visit,
I've been waiting in the west tower, how many full moons?

G W

Han Hong

Visiting a Daoist Temple

From the Tower of Immortals, I can see the Five Gateways;
the countryside is fresh and cool after rainfall in the night.
Distant mountains merge into woodlands close to Qin,
where autumn washboards sounded near the Han Palace.
In the stillness, a few pines cast shadows on the altar;
fine grasses send their fragrance from a secluded hollow.
What use is there in searching for a world beyond?
Here, within the human world, are the heavenly hills.

M E F

Huangfu Ran

Sad Thoughts in Spring

Orioles call and sparrows chatter, spring is here again;
Mayi Pass and Dragon's Mound, how many thousand miles away?
I live within the city walls, near the Emperor's gardens,
but my heart follows the bright moon into barbarian skies.
On my loom, I weave poems that tell my long-held sorrows;
on the tower, flowered branches mock me for sleeping alone.
So I ask the great cavalry general Dou Xian,
when will he return under flags of victory from Mount Yan?

GW

Lu Lun

Passing by Ezhou in the Evening

The clouds open and I see Hanyang city far in the distance,
still a day away for this little boat.
The traders slept this morning, knowing the river would be
    smooth;
the boatmen in the night whispered as the tide freshened.
Wandering these southern streams, my whiskers grew white as
    autumn;
under the moonlight, I think of home, ten thousand miles away.
All I had, all I hoped for, was destroyed in the rebellion;
unbearable, the sound of war drums rolls again across the river.

GW

Liu Zhongyuan

Climbing the Gate Tower at Liuzhou; Sent to the Governors of Zhang, Ding, Feng and Lian Prefectures

From this high tower, a view of wilderness;
a huge expanse of gloom between sea and sky.
A sudden wind-gust agitates the lotus in the moat;
heavy slanting rain invades the fig-trees on the wall.
There are mountains choked in woods to the far horizon;
the river makes nine curves like twisted bowels.
Stranded in this southern land of tattooed folk,
there's precious little likelihood of news from home.

MEF

Liu Yuxi

Thinking of the Past at West Pass Mountain

Wang Chun came downriver in his warships from Yizhou,
and the spirit of kings was extinguished at Jinling.
A thousand yards of chain sank to the bottom;
a flag of surrender rose above Stone City.
Witness to human suffering through the ages,
the mountain still stands guard at the river crossing.
Now, we are one nation between four rivers;
only autumn reeds whisper among these ruins.

GW

Yuan Zhen

Elegy (1)

Like Duke Xie's youngest, most beloved daughter,
you married me, a poor Qin Lou, and our life was hard.
When I had nothing to wear, you hunted through our hamper;
when I had no wine, you pawned your golden pins.
You foraged wild plants and sweet bean shoots for us to eat,
found dead leaves for fuel, watching old scholar-trees for their fall.
Today, I am rich, a hundred thousand a year,
and all I can do is leave these offerings for your soul.

GW

Elegy (2)

Remember the day we joked about what happens after death?
This morning, I see it all come true before my eyes.
I give away your clothes, they're almost gone;
I kept your needlework, but I cannot bear to open the little box
    that holds it.
I still remember the feelings we shared, so I'm kind to your maids;
sometimes, in dreams, I burn money at your grave.
I know all of us must someday feel the grief of loss,
but, poor as we two were, we had so few happy times.

GW

Elegy (3)

I sit here, grieving for the two of us;
how much of life's span remains for me?
Deng You lost his son and railed at destiny;
Pan Yue mourned his wife, composing futile verses.
Shall we share a hollow in the netherworld,

171

or reborn, meet in some other troubled life?
All night long, my eyes will see once more
your brow's deep furrows, carved by a life of care.

MEF

Bai Juyi

Untitled

Following the upheavals in Henan and the famine in Guannei district, my brothers were scattered, each in a different place. At full moon I was moved to express my thoughts and send this to my elder brother in Fuliang, my seventh brother in Yuqian, my fifteenth brother in Niaojiang, also to be shown to my younger brothers and sisters in Fuli and Xiagui.

In this disastrous year of famine, we lost everything,
my brothers all exiled, scattered east and west.
The country devastated in the aftermath of war,
flesh and blood forced out, to roam the streets.
I mourn my shadow, lost to the wandering wild goose.
Fragile plants are blown away, torn from their roots.
We each look at the same moon through flowing tears,
one night, five places, the same sickness in our hearts.

MEF

Li Shangyin

The Patterned Lute

No special reason the patterned lute has fifty strings,
each string, each fret, a reminder of better times.
Master Zhuang awoke from his dream, bewildered butterfly;
King Wang's love lives on in the cuckoo's cry.
The moon shines over the great ocean, pearls weep;
the sun warms Blue Mountain, jade smokes.
This feeling might have lasted forever in my memory,
but in the moment it was already fading away.

GW

Untitled

Last night's stars, last night's winds,
west of the Painted Chamber, east of the Laurel Hall.
Although not blessed with rainbow Phoenix wings,
we've learned to fly the space between our hearts.
Across the table, we played hide-the hook with spring wine's warmth;
in teams, we turned to guessing-games as candles burned red.
Too bad! The palace drum called me back to duty:
horseback to Orchid Terrace, chaotic tumbleweed.

MEF

The Sui Emperor's Palace

His palace, with its purple moat, was locked in mist and fog;
how he longed to make Yangzhou his new capital.
If Heaven had not passed its Mandate to founders of the Tang,
his brocade sails could have carried him to the ends of the earth.
Now, no fireflies rise from mounds of rotting grass;
only raucous crows nest in the old willows he planted.

If he should meet the last ruler of Chen in the afterlife,
would he ask to hear again the old song, "Flowers in the Rear
    Courtyard"?

GW

Untitled

Empty promises: you're gone without a trace;
the moon sinks past the tower at the fifth watch.
I dreamed our final parting, stifled a cry,
scratched out this letter, the ink still damp.
The candle's half-reflected in our kingfisher-quilt;
the embroidered flowers hold a trace of your perfume.
Emperor Wu came to regret the distance to the Celestial Peak:
our pathway's blocked by untold other mountains.

MEF

Untitled

The east wind whispers, fine rain begins;
beyond the lotus pool, faint sounds of thunder.
Where the gold toad bites the lock, smoke from incense curls;
where the jade tiger holds the silken rope, the well-hoist turns.
Mistress Jia peeped through the curtain at young Secretary Han;
Lady Fu bequeathed her pillow to the Prince of Wei.
Spring hearts should not compete with blossoming flowers—
for each inch of lovers' yearning, an inch of ash.

MEF

At the Staging Post of "Preparing the Brush"

Apes and birds still tremble, fearing your commands;
wind and clouds still gather to protect your stronghold.
As commander-in chief, you wielded a lively brush,
but your King rode a wagon to captivity.
Your skills topped those of Guan and Yue,
but how did your captains come to die so soon?
Although a temple was built in your old hometown,
the Liangfu Lament is your true memorial.

MEF

Untitled

It is hard for us to meet, harder still to part;
the east wind can't halt the flowers' decay.
The spring silkworm spins till death ends his thread;
the candle drips tears till its wick is ash.
At the morning mirror she grieves that her hair will gray;
reciting poems at night, she feels moonlight's chill.
Peng Mountain, home of immortals, is not far away—
may a bluebird tell her how I long to see her!

DL

Spring Rain

Spring is beginning; fitful sleep in a thick white robe;
of Baimen, no trace now, so much sadness since then.
I stood in the rain, watching your red tower;
the lamp and curtains of my carriage sway as I go home alone.
In spring sunset on this long road, are you as sad as I am?
After a long night, I finally catch a glimpse of you in dreams.
Jade earrings, sealed letter—how can I send them?
A thousand miles of clouds, and only one goose flying.

GW

Untitled

Phoenix-tail silk, so fragrant and delicate:
deep at night, she sews a green bed-curtain.
Her moon-shaped fan could not conceal her shame,
as his carriage thundered off with no pledge spoken.
Alone once more, she watches the candle's gold grow dim.
No word came; pomegranate wine remains unpoured.
Somewhere, his piebald horse is tied to a weeping willow;
where can she find an obliging southwest wind?

MEF

Untitled

Under heavy drapes, deep in the Hall of Forget Your Sorrow,
she passes the long night in fragile, fretful sleep.
The lifetime of a goddess drifts by in a dream,
as if she were a maiden still, back home without a man.
Storms are heedless of the caltrop's delicate stalks,
the cassia by nature yields its scent to morning dew.
Although it's said that suffering for love is futile,
what harm is melancholy and a little madness?

MEF

Wen Tingyun

The Southern Ferry Dock at Lizhou

Slanting sunlight sets in the clear water;
the curved island fades into blue misty hills.
On the shore, a horse whinnies as the boat sets out;
across the stream, people wait under willow trees for its return.
A flock of gulls breaks from tussocks on the sandy bank;
one heron soars above wide fields along the river.
Who could know I board this boat to search for Fan Li?
Only on misty lakes could he find solace from treason.

GW

Su Wu's Memorial Temple

Su Wu lived and died in the service of Han;
his temple, high among trees, commands wide views.
Wild geese have long abandoned moonlit skies of Hu,
sheep return to graze amid the mists of Gansu.
He had set out as a youth with cap and sword;
returning to the capital, he discovered all had changed:
the old Emperor dead at Maoling, he received no honors.
Tears for lost years flowed like the autumn river.

MEF

Xue Feng

In the Palace

In the Twelve Towers, made up and ready since morning,
they watch for their Prince from the Immortal's Lookout.
The door latch, a carved animal's head, hangs cold and silent;
from a dragon-shaped water clock, their day runs out slowly.
Cloud curls combed, again they check the mirror;
silk gowns ready, a little more perfume.
They look across to the main hall and watch through open blinds,
as uniformed palace maids prepare the Emperor's bed.

GW

Qin Taoyu

A Poor Woman

In her humble cottage, fragrant silks are things unknown.
She grieves that go-betweens refuse to help her,
for who would fall for homely skills and honesty?
Frugal dress and simple make-up gather only pity.
She can boast of agile fingers, clever with a needle,
but can't compete with painting comely eyebrows.
More desperate every year, she embroiders golden thread
on gorgeous bridal gowns for other girls to wear.

MEF

七律樂府
Seven-Word Regulated Yuefu

Shen Quanqi

Ancient Style Grievance Poem

A young wife known as Tulip lives in the House of Lu,
where pairs of swallows roost on beams of tortoiseshell.
In cold September, washboard drumming hastens falling leaves.
The Liaoyang Army ten years gone, she only has her memories.
No news or letters come from north of White Wolf River.
The autumn nights drag slowly by in Red Phoenix City.
Who can bear such grief alone, who is here to understand,
only the moon reflected on the shiny silk she weaves?

MEF

五言絕句
Five-word Quatrains

Wang Wei

At Deer Park Hermitage

Empty mountain, no one in sight—
yet an echo of voices;
Rays of sunset pierce deep forest,
again lighting blue-green mosses.

DL

Bamboo Refuge

Sitting alone in dense bamboo,
I play my lute and sing along.
In these deep woods, unknown to people,
the moon arrives; we shine together.

MEF

Farewell in the Mountains

Our farewells in the mountains are over;
with dusk coming on, I close my door.
Spring grass is green year after year,
but my friend I may see no more.

DL

Thinking of Each Other

Red sandalwood grows in that southern land;
when fall comes, the branches fill with seeds.
I hope you will gather as many as you can;
these, above all, will help you think of me.

GW

Impromptu Poem

You came from my old home town,
so you may know what's happening there.
The day you left, beneath my latticed window,
were the cold plums yet in flower?

GW

Pei Di

Farewell to Cui Xingzong

Going into the mountains, whether deep or not,
you should enjoy the beauty of hills and valleys.
But, don't be like that man from Wuling,
who only stayed a while at Peach Blossom Spring.

GW

Zu Yong

Looking at the Snow on South Mountain

The shady northern slopes of South Mountain are beautiful,
with snow piled up to the floating clouds.
The woods glow with that bright after-snow color;
in town, the nights are growing colder.

GW

Meng Haoran

Passing the Night on Jiande River

Anchor the boat in a mist-heavy cove;
day sinks into dusk, sadness rises.
Vast plain, sky touching treetops,
clear river, moon floating just out of reach.

DL

Spring Morning

Sleeping in spring, the sun rises before I do,
all around me the twittering of birds.
Rain patter on the roof, wind shrieking at night:
flower petals fell—who knows how many!

DL

Li Bai

Thoughts on a Quiet Night

Beside my bed, the bright moon lit the floor;
waking, at first I thought it was the frost.
I looked up to see the bright moon shining,
then bowed my head to think of home again.

GW

Sad Feelings

A beautiful woman raises her pearl blinds;
she sits in the dark and knits her brows.
Only wet traces of her tears are seen;
who knows for whom they are shed?

GW

Du Fu

The Eight Formations

Your achievements overshadowed any in the Three Kingdoms;
most famous of all was your design for the Eight Formations.
Against the river's surge, they stand solid, immovable,
a monument to your lasting regret at failing to swallow up Wu.

DL

Wang Zhihuan

Climbing Crane Tower

The white sun vanishes at the mountain-top;
the Yellow River is swallowed by the sea.
Wanting to see a thousand miles farther,
you climb one more flight of stairs.

DL

Liu Changqing

Farewell to Priest Ling Che

Secluded in its grove stands the Bamboo Forest Temple;
the sound of its bell comes muffled in the fading dusk.
Seeming to carry the last light on his straw hat,
he returns alone into the dark green hills of night.

GW

Listening to Someone Playing the Lute

In quiet chill, from the seven strings, there rises
the faint sound of a cool wind in the pines.
It is an old song and we both love it;
people these days rarely play it any more.

GW

Farewell to the Reverend Fang Wai

A lonely cloud sees off the wild crane—
"How could you stay in the world of men?
But crane, don't buy a mountain spot in Wozhou:
word has spread about how great it is."

GW

Wei Yingwu

Autumn Night: a Letter to Officer Qiu

Thinking of you this autumn night,
strolling, declaiming to the cold sky
among the falling pine-cones on an empty mountain.
Alone, like me, you won't be sleeping.

MEF

Li Duan

Listening to the Zither

She plays a zither made from cassia wood,
with her white hands, in a jade room.
Since she wants the young gentleman to notice her,
she plays a wrong note now and then.

GW

Wang Jian

A New Bride

On the third day, she enters the kitchen,
and washes her hands to prepare the first soup.
She doesn't know yet how her mother-in-law likes it,
so she gives her husband's sister the first taste.

GW

Quan Deyu

In the "Jade Terrace" Style

Last night, the sash of my robe came loose;
this morning, spiders are weaving webs.
I still have some make-up I couldn't throw away;
do these omens mean my husband will at last come home?

GW

Liu Zhongyuan

River Snow

Endless mountains, no birds fly;
no footprint traces on a thousand paths.
One boat, an old man in rush cape and bamboo hat,
alone, fishing, in cold river snow.

MEF

Yuan Zhen

The Summer Palace

Lonely and run down stands the old summer palace,
around it the royal flowers, lonely and red.
White-haired, the palace women lounge there at ease;
they exchange old gossip of an emperor long dead.

DL

Bai Juyi

Invitation to Liu Nineteen

I have some unfiltered wine, "green-ant" fresh,
and a little red clay warming-stove.
Evening is falling, and the sky looks like snow.
Can you drink a cup with me, or no?

DL

Zhang Hu

Master He's Tune

My old home is a thousand miles away;
I've been confined to the palace for twenty years.
As I sang the first sad notes of "Master He's Tune,"
before the Emperor, two teardrops fell.

GW

Li Shangyin

Climbing Leyou Heights

Toward nightfall, ill at ease,
I urge my carriage up the ancient heights.
The evening sun has boundless beauty,
but now, it is about to set.

GW

Jia Dao

Seeking a Hermit but Not Finding Him

Beneath the pines, I asked his servant boy—
"The Master is gone, out picking medicinal herbs.
He's somewhere in these mountains,
deep in the clouds, but I couldn't say where."

DL

Li Pin

Crossing the Han River

Beyond those southern peaks, no news or letters;
I was gone a winter and again a spring down there.
Now nearing home, I grow a little nervous,
afraid to question people I meet along the way.

GW

Jin Changxu

Spring Grievance

Scare away the yellow orioles;
make them stop singing, up in the branches.
When they sing, it ruins a wife's dreaming;
only dreams can take her west of the Liao.

GW

Anonymous Soldier in the West

A Song of Geshu Han

As the seven stars of the Dipper shine on him,
Geshu Han carries his sword at night.
The Tibetans have gone south with their herds of horses,
afraid to venture past Linyao.

GW

Cui Hao

Changan Song (1)

"Sir, where is your family from?
I come from Hengtang.
Stop your boat awhile so I can ask you,
because I think we may be from the same town."

G W

Changan Song (2)

"My house overlooks the water of Nine Rivers;
we come and go between the Nine Rivers' shores.
We are both from Changan;
I guess in our whole lives we never met till now."

G W

Li Bai

Jade Stairs Grievance

On the jade stairs, white dew is born—
the night is long, the dew invades her silk stockings.
She steps inside and lowers the crystal-strung curtain;
through glittering jewels, she stares at the autumn moon.

D L

Lu Lun

At the Frontier (1)

Vulture feathers tip his golden arrows;
swallowtail ribbons decorate his bow.
Standing tall, he alone gives new commands,
to one great cheer from a thousand campfires.

MEF

At the Frontier (2)

The forest is dark, grass rustles in the breeze;
the general, in the night, stretches his bow.
The next morning, they find the white feathered arrow,
sunk in the cleft of a stone.

GW

At the Frontier (3)

The moon is dark, geese fly high;
the Chanyu eluded us in the night.
Our light cavalry harried their retreat,
heavy snow covering their bows and swords.

GW

At the Frontier (4)

In our camp beyond the wastes, there is feasting everywhere;
even the barbarians celebrate our triumphal return.
Drunk together, in our golden armor, we dance;
our drums thunder over rivers and mountains.

GW

Li Yi

A Southern Tune

I married a Qutang trader;
day after day, he breaks his promise to come home.
I've always known how regular the tides are;
I should have married one who rides them.

_G W_

七言絕句
Seven-Word Quatrain

He Zhizhang

Written Impromptu on Returning Home

As a young boy, I left home; I return an old man.
My accent is still the same, but my temple hair is gray.
The children see me but don't know who I am;
laughing, they say, "Stranger, where are you from?"

G W

Zhang Xu

Peach Blossom Creek

A wooden bridge, hanging in the mist, to some obscure far shore.
Beneath a rocky cliff, I ask the fisherman in his boat to tell me:
"These peach blossom petals floating endlessly on the current;
do they come from that old cave with its clear flowing water?"

G W

Wang Wei

On the Ninth Day of the Ninth Month, Remembering My Brothers East of the Mountain

Alone, a traveler in a foreign land,
I miss my family twice as much when a holiday passes.
Back there, I know my brothers are climbing a hill;
this year, there's one fewer to gather dogwood.

GW

Wang Changling

At the Hibiscus Tower, Farewell to Xin Jian

Cold rain crossed the river the night we entered Wu;
now, in the dawn, I send you on alone through the mountains of Chu.
When you get back to Luoyang, if my friends should ask about me,
tell them my heart is still pure: an ice crystal in a jade vase.

GW

Boudoir Lament

Secure in her boudoir, a young wife knew no sorrow,
until, dressed for spring, she climbed the emerald staircase.
At the sight of willows by the roadside, freshly green:
a pang of regret that she sent him off to be a hero.

MEF

194

Spring in the Palace

In last night's wind, the peach by the well opened its flowers;
the moon rose like a bright wheel above the Weiyang Palace.
After the singing and dancing at Pingyang's, the Emperor found
    his favorite,
and gave her a brocade robe against the spring chill.

GW

Wang Han

Liangzhou

Wine from grapes, in cups white as the moon,
as soon as we drink, the lute summons us to attack.
If I end up drunk on some sandy battlefield, don't laugh;
since ancient times, gone to war, how many have come back?

GW

Li Bai

Seeing Meng Haoran Off from Yellow Crane Tower

From Yellow Crane Tower my old friend leaves;
in the flower-mists of April he heads down to Yangrou.
Lonely sail, distant silhouette, he disappears into blue emptiness;
I see only the long river flowing to the edge of heaven.

DL

Leaving Early from White Emperor City

We left White Emperor among dawn-reddened clouds.
A thousand miles to Jiangling, crossed in a day!
From both riverbanks, the constant shriek of gibbons;
already our small boat has passed a thousand serried mountains.

DL

Cen Shen

Meeting a Courier en Route to the Capital

If I look eastward toward my old home, the road is much too long;
my sleeves are soaked, my tears will not stop falling.
We met on horseback, no paper or ink or brushes,
so I ask you just to carry my words: tell them I am safe.

GW

Du Fu

Meeting Li Guinian in the South

At the home of the Prince of Qi, I have often seen you,
and in the hall of Cui Jiu, I have heard you sing.
Truly these southlands boast unrivalled scenery—
to see you once again when the flowers are falling.

DL

Wei Yingwu

On the West Bank of the Chuzhou Gorge

I love the shaded grass that grows beside the gorge;
above it, yellow orioles chirp deep in the woods.
The spring flood, swelled by rain, flows faster at evening;
at this deserted ferry, one must get the boat across alone.

G W

Zhang Ji (2)

Moored at Night by Maple Bridge

The moon sinks, crows call, frost fills the sky;
maples on the bank, fishermen's lamps, my sad half-sleep.
Beyond Suzhou lies Cold Mountain Temple—
its midnight bell sounds in the traveler's boat.

D L

Han Hong

Cold Food Day

In this spring city, flowers are flying everywhere;
on Cold Food Day, an east wind bends willows by the moat.
At dusk, the Han Palace sends out wax candles;
their smoke floats first into noble houses.

G W

Liu Fangping

Moonlit Night

Late at night, the moon floods light on half my house;
the North Dipper's high above, the South Dipper sinks from sight.
Tonight I feel the warmth of spring begin to stir,
as insects whisper through green window shades.

MEF

Spring Sadness

Through her curtains, she watches the sunset and the fading dusk;
in her golden room, none see the stains her tears have made.
In a deserted courtyard, where spring is almost over,
pear blossoms fill the ground outside a door she never opens.

GW

Liu Zhongyong

Grievance of One on a Campaign

Year after year, the Golden River; again, the Jade Pass;
each morning, the horsewhip and the sword.
Late spring, and snow returns to her green grave mound;
the long Yellow River flows on around Black Mountain.

GW

Gu Kuang

In the Palace

From the tall Jade Tower rises the song of a flute;
carried on the wind, the palace ladies' happy chatter.
In Moon Hall, shadows lengthen, a water-clock drips,
crystal blinds raised to watch the autumn river.

G W

Li Yi

Climbing the Wall at Shouxiang by Night, Hearing a Flute

Below the peaks at Huile, the sand is like snow;
outside the walls of Shouxiang, moonlight like frost.
I don't know where he plays his simple flute,
but all through the night, our soldiers think of home.

G W

Liu Yuxi

Crow Robe Alley

By Redbird Bridge, wild plants flower;
outside Crow Robe Alley, the evening sun slants.
Swallows that nested by noblemen's mansions,
now fly into houses of the common people.

G W

Spring Song

Freshly adorned, down from the Vermilion Chamber.
deep in spring's embrace, she wanders sadly round the courtyard.
As she stands among the flowers, counting them,
a dragonfly settles on her jade hairpin.

MEF

Bai Juyi

Concubine's Song

Tears soak her silk scarf; dreams are out of reach.
Deep at night, from the Royal Chamber, comes the sound of
    singing.
Young and lovely, but rejected,
she crouches by the incense burner, silent, waiting for the dawn.

MEF

Zhang Hu

Given to a Woman in the Palace

Behind a forbidden gate, moonlight moves through palace trees;
her beautiful eyes watch swallows sleeping in their nests.
She pulls out her jade hairpins, lamplight her companion,
trims the wicks, sets a trapped moth free to fly.

GW

On the Terrace of Gathered Spirits (1)

Sunlight slants across the Terrace of Gathered Spirits;
red flowers open to welcome the morning dew.
Last night the Emperor issued a new order;
Yang Guifei smiled to herself as she came through his curtains.

GW

On the Terrace of Gathered Spirits (2)

The Consort-of-State Guo received her Master's favor;
at dawn, she galloped a horse through the palace gates.
Because she felt make-up obscured her natural beauty,
she wiped it off before entering the Emperor's presence.

GW

Written on the Jinling Ferry-crossing

At Jinling, there is a small inn by the ferry dock;
a traveler spends the night there, full of sadness.
When the tide turns, under a setting moon,
in the distance, two or three lights flicker at Guazhou.

GW

Zhu Qingyu

Palace Poem

Silence; palace gates imprison palace flowers:
lovelies standing side-by-side along the jade veranda.
They'd love to talk about the Palace goings-on,
but, with the parrot close by, they dare not say a word.

MEF

Thoughts from the Women's Apartments, Offered to Minister of Waterways and Irrigation Zhang Ji

Red candles burned all night in the bridal chamber;
at dawn, she must go to the front hall to greet her husband's
    parents.
Her makeup finished, she whispers to her husband,
"The way I've done my eyebrows, is it still in fashion?"

GW

Du Mu

About to Leave for Wuxing, I Climb the Leyou Plateau

In such a beautiful season, I'd like to take time off, but can't;
with leisure, under these lonely clouds, I could live in peace like
    a monk.
But before I raise my Prefect's pennant and head off to my new
    post,
I climb the Leyou Plateau, for one last look at Emperor Taizong's
    tomb.

GW

Red Cliff

A broken spear sunk in sand, its iron still not rusted;
I pick it up, clean it, and remember the old kingdoms.
If the east wind had not favored General Zhou,
that spring, two wives would have remained imprisoned.

GW

Moored on the Qin Huai River

Smoke blankets cold water, moonlight blankets sand,
moored at night on the Qin Huai near a wine-shop,
where the singing-girl doesn't know the grief of a fallen nation—
across the river she still sings "Flowers of the Inner Court."

DL

Sent to Administrative Assistant Han Chuo at Yangzhou

The blue mountains are dark, the water vast and wide;
autumn is finished down in the South, but the grass has not yet
    died.
On the twenty-four bridges of Yangzhou, this moonlit night,
where are you teaching some girl to play the flute?

GW

Sharing My Feelings

Dissatisfied, I wandered rivers and lakes, drinking as I went;
slim-waisted girls of Chu, so light they danced in my palm.
Ten years later, I awoke from my Yangzhou dream,
known only for breaking hearts in green towers.

GW

Mid-Autumn Night

A silver candle in autumn lights the cold painted screen;
a light silk fan beats, fireflies flow around it.
In my courtyard, the night sky is clear as water;
I sit and watch Herdboy and Weaver Girl meet.

GW

Given in Parting (1)

A girl so light and graceful, barely thirteen,
like a fresh nutmeg on the branch in the second month.
For ten miles in a spring breeze, along the boulevards of Yangzhou,
though all the women raised their blinds, you were most beautiful.

GW

Given in Parting (2)

Too much emotion is like none at all,
as I wait with my wine for the smile that will not come.
Candles have hearts, are sad for us at partings;
their tears, instead of mine, drip till the sky brightens.

GW

The Garden of the Golden Valley

All the extravagance of those days has vanished with the fragrant
    dust;
the river flows by without caring now, the gardens gone to seed.
At dusk, an east wind carries the sad sounds of birds;
as flowers fall, so from this tower she fell for love.

GW

Li Shangyin

Night Rain, Sent North

You ask when I'm coming home; I don't know yet.
Here in the Ba Mountains, night rain overflows the lakes in
    autumn.
When will we sit together, trimming wicks in the western
    window,
talking about these night rains in the Ba Mountains?

GW

Message to Secretary Linghu

Clouds of Song Shan, trees of Qin, far behind me now,
I've penned this message for a pair of carp to carry:
Don't ask this old habitué of Liang Gardens
how sick he feels in these Maoling autumn rains.

MEF

There Is Only

There is only, behind the mica screen, a beautiful woman;
winter is over in the capital, she dreads these new spring nights.
If she hadn't married such a high-ranking husband,
he wouldn't leave their perfumed bed to serve at Morning
    Audience.

GW

The Sui Palace

He mounted his carriage and traveled south, took no special
    precautions,
ignoring boxes of memorials that urged him not to go.
In the spring wind, the whole kingdom made brocades for the
    palace;
half he used for mud flaps, half for sails.

GW

Jasper Lake

By Jasper Lake, the Queen Mother of the West throws open her
    silken curtains;
the "Yellow Bamboo Song" sounds, with its grief that moves the
    world.
His eight steeds could run thirty thousand miles a day,
so why hasn't King Mu come back to her again?

GW

Chang E

On her mica screen, candlelight flickers, fading;
the River of Stars gradually sets, the dawn star engulfed.
Chang E should regret stealing the elixir of eternal life;
in the azure sea, in the green blue heaven, night after night her
    heart.

GW

Master Jia

The palace sought sages, recalled the exiled statesman
Master Jia, whose talents were beyond all others.
How sad, at midnight, when he moved his mat closer,
the Emperor asked not about men, but about ghosts.

GW

Wen Tingyun

Jade Lute Reproach

Icy bamboo mat, silver bed, dreams won't come;
jade green sky like water, a few night clouds.
Cries of a distant wild goose passing over Xiang river.
Twelve empty towers, the woman and the moon.

MEF

Zheng Tian

Mawei Slope

The Bright Emperor wheeled his horse to ride away, the Yang
    Consort dead;
their love was unforgettable, but time passes and renews.
After all, it was the wise, the Imperial thing to do;
better than that other Emperor, who saved his concubines but
    lost his kingdom.

GW

Han Wo

Already Cool

Beyond the blue railing, woven blinds hang,
a red screen embroidered with broken willows.
On eight-foot dragon beard mats, a square brocade cushion;
the weather is already cool, but it is still too soon for cold.

G W

Wei Zhuang

A Picture of Jinling

Rain falls on the river in sheets, the grassy bank is lush;
the Six Dynasties are like a dream, birds call in the emptiness.
Unmoved, willows hang over the terrace wall;
as then, flowers like mist over the Ten-mile Dike.

G W

Chen Tao

Ballad of the Border

Sworn to sweep away the Xiongnu tribes, or die trying,
five thousand marched out in brocade and marten fur—all lie in
    Tartar dust.
Have pity for these bones beside Shifting River,
whose flesh still lives in spring bedchamber dreams.

D L

Zhang Bi

Sent to a Friend

After you left, I dreamed of visiting your home:
the tiny hallway, the curving balustrade,
but there was only the spring moon over the courtyard,
shining on fallen blossoms for one no longer there.

MEF

Anonymous

Anonymous Poem

Cold Food Day is near, rain has made the grass grow lush;
barley shoots sway in a breeze, green willows line the dyke.
We both have homes, but cannot yet return;
cuckoo, stop repeating those words in my ear!*

GW

---

*The cuckoo traditionally says, "Buru Gui": "It's better to go home."

七言絕句樂府
Seven-Word Quatrain Yuefu

Wang Wei

Wei City Song

Morning rain wets the light dust in Wei city;
willows spring green, so green beside the guest house.
Let's drain another wine cup—
west of the Yang Pass no old friend awaits you.

DL

Autumn Night

The moon begins to wax, the autumn dew is light;
her dress is too sheer, but she does not change it.
All night she plays her silver lute, absorbed, possessed,
depressed by her empty room, unwilling to return.

GW

Wang Changling

Grievance in the Ever-Faithful Palace

I sweep the courtyard as dawn brightens, open the golden hall,
then pick up a discarded fan and linger here awhile.
My beauty must not even be a match for those cold crows,
flying back from the Zhaoyang Palace, still warm from its sun.

GW

Crossing the Frontier

The moon as it was in Qin, the pass as it was in Han;
soldiers marched ten thousand miles, they never returned.
If only the Flying General was still at Dragon City,
he could stop these Tartar horsemen from crossing the Shadow
    Mountains.

GW

Wang Zhihuan

Crossing the Border

The Yellow River merges into white clouds far away;
a small deserted town sits high at the mountain top.
That Tartar flute should not be playing the *Willow Tree Lament*;
spring breezes never blow this way through Jade Gate Pass.

MEF

Li Bai

Clear and Bright Tunes (1)

The clouds remind me of her dress, the flowers of her face;
a spring breeze moves the trellis, peonies sweet with dew.
Even if I had not seen her up on Many Jades Peak,
here, under the moon on this jeweled terrace, we would surely
    meet.

GW

Clear and Bright Tunes (2)

One twig of red peony, scent captured in this pure night's dew,
the clouds and rain of the Lady of Mount Wu, sad for no reason.
May I ask, who in all the Han palaces could have been her match?
Even less, Zhao Feiyan in her finest makeup.

GW

Clear and Bright Tunes (3)

The most famous flower, the most beautiful woman, each
    admires the other;
whenever their King looks at them, he cannot help but smile.
So he lets go of that sad feeling the spring breezes bring,
and leans against the north railing sunk in their perfume.

GW

Miss Du Qiu

Clothes from Golden Thread

Please, sir, don't prize a robe of golden thread;
please, sir, treasure your youthful years.
When blossoms open on a branch, then break it off:
don't wait until the branch is bare!

GW

Notes to the Poems

Afterthoughts 1–4 (pp. 37–38): These four allegorical poems were written after Zhang Jiuling was banished in 737 following a dispute with the Court.

Sad Thoughts in Spring (p. 40): Written ca. 740, in the voice of a woman waiting for her man to return home.

Gazing at Mount Tai (p. 41): Written in 736. Mount Tai is in Shandong province. It is one of the five sacred mountains of Daoist tradition, and has been a destination for pilgrims for at least 3,000 years.

Poem for Wei Ba (p. 41): Written in the spring of 759.

Dreaming of Li Bai (1) (p. 43): "Nets of the law" refers to legal troubles after the failed coup of Prince Yong.
   The souls of the living were believed to travel from the body at times of unconsciousness.

A Farewell (p. 45): Addressed to Wang Wei's friend Meng Haoran, who had just failed the Imperial examination. Filled with shame, Meng exiled himself from society.

Farmers on Wei River (p. 46): Silkworms sleep before casting off their cocoons. The *Ode* referred to is #36 from the *Book of Odes*, which begins: "It cannot be, it cannot be; / So, why not return? / Were we not in service to our Lord, / Why would we be out here on the road?"

A Song for Xi Shi (p. 47): Xi Shi was a great beauty who is believed to have lived near the end of the Spring and Autumn period (8-3rd Century BCE). It is said that her characteristic frown was due to chest pains, but her look of suffering was considered a beautiful attribute and was widely imitated by would-be beauties.

With My Cousin . . . (p. 50): The last line alludes to Cui's excellent reputation, known widely, in spite of his low-ranking post in the south.

Encountering Feng Zhu in the Capital (p. 56): This poem has been interpreted as a criticism of Feng Zhu for wasting his talent outside of government; or is Wei Yingwu simply envious?

Dwelling Beside a Stream (p. 59): Written during Liu Zongyuan's exile in Yongzhou.

Song of the Border (1) (p. 60): The "inner plains" are in the Hebei-Shanxi region.

Song of the Border (2) (p. 60): Lin Tau was where the Great Wall began.

Spring (p. 62): The last line alludes to an old poem from the Han called *Mulberries on the Levee* that has the lines, "The official comes from the South, / his five horses hesitate."

Summer (p. 62): Xi Shi: see note for p. 47. Mirror Lake is near Shaoxing, in Zhejiang province.

A Song of Changan (p. 63): Ezra Pound's masterpiece rings in the ears of every translator who attempts this poem.

Song of a Lute (p. 67): The Guangling San was an ancient collection of melodies in a very impassioned style, reputedly based on stories from the Warring States period (475–255 BCE).

On Hearing Dong Tinglan Play . . . (p. 67): In the last line of the poem, Li is watching for Dong to arrive at the Palace, where he was often a guest.

Listening to An Wanshan Play . . . (p. 69): The reed whistle is called a *bili*; it is shaped like a flute with 8 or 9 holes; it emits a mournful sound produced by a reed. It is native to Central Asia and was imported to China during the Han border wars.

My Dream of Visiting Mount Tianyu (p. 72): Mt. Tianmu is in Zhejiang province. Tianmu means "old lady of the heavens." The name originates from a legend in which a climber heard an old woman singing on the mountaintop.

A Ballad of Running Horse Creek (p. 75): Running Horse Creek, Wheel Terrace, and Gold Mountain were all places in East Turkestan, the area now the Xinjiang Uighur Autonomous Region. Feng Changqing was a Tang Dynasty general who was successful in the battle described in this poem, but was later executed for treason when he failed to defeat An Lushan in the rebellion of 755.

A Song of Wheel Terrace (p. 76): The "urgent message," would have been in the form of a communication written on a slip of wood with a feather attached to indicate its urgency.

At Office Manager Wei Feng's House . . . (p. 78): General Cao Ba was a descendant of the famous Han Dynasty general Cao Cao.

A Song of Painting . . . (p. 79): The Gallery of Famous Men: the Taizong Emperor hung portraits of the twenty-four greatest generals, who helped him found the dynasty, in the Pavilion of Surpassing the Clouds.

Sent to Grand Master of Remonstrance Han Zhu (p. 80): Written in 767. Han Zhu served under the Suzong Emperor and assisted him in his efforts to recover the Capital from the An Lushan rebels. Later, he became disillusioned with the Emperor's policies and retired to his home at Yueyang in present-day Hunan.

The "spirits around the big dipper" refers to the high-ranking officials gathering around the Emperor in Changan. The Sages, literally winged ones or immortals, are faithful ministers like Han, who left government service to avoid compromising their principles.

Sima Tan, father of Sima Qian, was Grand Historian at the Han court. In 110 BCE he was left behind when the Emperor went into the countryside to inaugurate an important sacrifice. He fell ill and died soon afterwards, leaving the historical material he had collected to his son, who finished the *Shi Ji*, or *Records of the Grand Historian* that his father had begun.

The Ancient Cypress (p. 81): The old cypress is at the Zhuge Liang Temple in Kuizhou, later Fengjie, now destroyed by the Three Gorges Reservoir. Wu Gorge, and Min Peak are in Sichuan. Brocade Pavilion is in Chengdu. Du Fu had built a small pavilion beside the Brocade River near his thatched cottage outside Chengdu.

Gongming is a courtesy name for Zhuge Liang (181–234 C.E.), who served as Minister to Liu Bei, King of Shu (now Sichuan), the First Ruler mentioned later. Zhuge Liang was legendary in China for his brilliance, loyalty and resourcefulness—the kind of statesman Du Fu thought was needed in his own time. The temple was built next to the cypress reputed to have been planted by his own hand.

The Phoenix is the Bird of Inspiration.

Arthur Cooper points out that the Chinese word for "timber" is exactly the same in sound and etymology as the word for "talent."

A Ballad . . . (p. 82): Line 5: "Yi" is the legendary Yi the Archer, a celestial being who was called upon by a king to chase away nine of the ten suns who were sporting in the sky, burning the land and causing drought and suffering. Yi became so angry that he shot down nine suns with his red bow, finally restoring the earth to fertility under one remaining sun.

Visiting Mount Heng . . . (p. 87): The Five Sacred Mountains of the Daoist tradition were: Song Mountain at the center, with Mounts Heng (Bei), Tai, Heng (Nan), and Hua, at north, east, south and west respectively. They were not close together, but spread over the length and breadth of China. Han Yu was visiting the southern Mount Heng, in today's Hunan province.

The Three Dukes were the three highest officials in the Tang Dynasty Administration, second in rank only to the Emperor.

Nearly 300 years later, the celebrated Song Dynasty scholar-poet Su Shi had a similar epiphany to that of Han Yu when he witnessed a spectacular mirage off the coast of Shandong. It inspired him to write a poem which alludes to this poem and even adopts Han Yu's structure and many of his rhymes. However, Su is more skeptical, and treats Han's assertion that the gods had responded to his "honesty and virtue" with scorn. Instead, Su comments: "How could he know that the gods took pity on his old age?"

The Song of Endless Sorrow (p. 92): Li Longji, born in 685 CE, became known as Ming Huang, the Bright Emperor. In 710, the reigning Emperor suddenly died and his Empress took control of the palace, placing her young son on the throne. Li Longji soon led an insurrection to assassinate her and her followers, placing his own father on the throne. The following year he became Regent, relegating his father to the role of figurehead, and succeeded his father on the throne in 712. His long reign saw the Tang Empire reach the height of its brilliance, and after 740, the beginning of its decline. In his later years, he fell under the influence of the powerful eunuch faction at court, aided by the family of his notorious concubine, Yang Guifei.

Yang Yuhuan was born in 719. She is usually known by her highest official title, Honored Consort Yang (Yang Guifei). In 735, she entered the palace as a concubine of Prince Shou, one of the Bright Emperor's sons, but within a few years, she became the Bright Emperor's own favorite. In 745, she received the title Honored Consort. She used her influence to promote the careers of many of her relatives, including her cousin, the incompetent and vicious Yang Guozhong.

General An Lushan, taking advantage of the seventy-year-old Bright Emperor's obsession, launched a rebellion in 755 that tore the Empire apart. In the summer of 756, the rebels captured the capital, Changan (the modern Xi'an). The Emperor and his retinue fled southwest toward the city of Chengdu in Shu, now part of Sichuan. About thirty miles west of the capital, at the Mawei post station, his army commanders refused to continue unless he allowed them to put Yang Guifei to death. The Emperor had no choice but to agree. She was strangled by a eunuch. Yang Guozhong and her notorious sister, the Consort-of-State Guo, were also executed on the spot. Before his party arrived in Chengdu, the Bright Emperor's third son replaced him on the throne. After the new Emperor's forces recaptured Changan in 757, the former Emperor returned from Shu to Changan, where he lived in seclusion until his death in 762.

Bai Juyi wrote this poem a few generations later, and it remains a deeply ingrained part of Chinese popular culture even today. It sets the story in the earlier Han Dynasty, but no reader could doubt who the real characters were.

Song of Yan (p. 102): This is a song from the Music Bureau (*yuefu*). Yan was the name of a state in North China until the beginning of the Han Dynasty. (The area is now in Hebei Province).

General Li: According to the Historical Records of Sima Qian, Li Guang was a respected Han military leader nicknamed "The Flying General." He came from Youbeiping near the Rehe River, now in northern Hebei Province. Although he narrowly defeated the Xiong Nu at the Battle of Mobei in 119 BCE, he was criticized for losing time by getting lost in the desert and for allowing Shanyu, the Xiongnu leader, to escape. Rather than return to Youbeiping in disgrace, he committed suicide.

An Old Soldier's Ballad (p. 103): The title is another Music Bureau tune. Jiaohe is in Xinjiang, near Turfan. The princess was Wang Zhaojun, from the Han Dynasty, one of the legendary Four Beauties of China. She was given to a chief of the Xiongnu as a token of peace, playing sad tunes on her lute as she traveled the long road, and passing through Jade Gate Pass in western Gansu. "Light Chariots" is another reference to Han General Li Guang. The grapevines were probably tribute given to the Han generals by the Xiongnu during the ensuing truce which lasted some 60 years.

Ballad of a Luoyang Girl (p. 104): This is one of Wang Wei's earliest known poems, probably composed when he was still in his teens.

The Hard Road to Shu (p. 108): Shu is now Sichuan Province. This area is separated from the rest of China by a continuous line of mountains with perilous passes. The translator happened to be working on this poem during the devastating 2008 earthquake in Sichuan. He was deeply impressed by the tenacity and organizational skill which resulted in rescue teams and heavy equipment reaching the victims quickly in spite of the difficulty of access, avoiding an even more disastrous outcome.

Endless Longing (1) & (2) (p. 110): These two poems complement each other; both express longing, the first in the voice of a man, the second in that of a woman.

Hard Road (3) (p. 112): A catalog of reluctant or unfortunate officials, adding up to a powerful argument for opting out!

Yingshui waters: a reference to Xu You, a valued subject of ancient Emperor Yao, who wanted him for high office. Xu, however, didn't want to hear, so he filled his ears with water from the Yingshui River.

Shouyang ferns: possibly refers to Zhen Zizhen of the Han Dynasty, who, rather than become an official, became a hermit, living in the mountains and surviving on plants.

Qu Yuan was a celebrated poet and statesman of the Warring States period. Like many before and since, he was banished from office several times in the wake of political power struggles. His warning to the court on appeasing the Qin was ignored, and when the state was overrun by the Qin army in 278 BCE, he threw himself into the river Miluo. Tradition has it that boats raced to rescue him, but failed; this is said to be the origin of the Dragon Boat Festival.

Lu Ji was a prominent scholar-statesman of the Kingdom of Wu. He was suspected to be guilty of treason and executed in the year 303 CE.

Li Si was a powerful minister under the First Emperor Qin Shi Huangdi. He was an influential advocate of the Legalist near-totalitarian system of government. After the death of the First Emperor, the new Emperor's chief eunuch, bent on establishing his own power-base, persuaded the Emperor to execute Li by cutting him in half in public.

Please Bring Wine! (p. 113): "Master Cen" is Cen Shen, a contemporary of Li Bai, a scholar-official who was called on to fight during the An Lushan rebellion. "Please bring wine" may be an allusion to Cen's quatrain written while serving in the army, which has the lines "If only I could climb somewhere / but no one sends me wine" (translation by Red Pine).

Ballad of the Army Carts (p. 115): Direct criticism of the Emperor or government policy was ill-advised. This poem, like many others, disguises comments about the current situation with references to ancient times.

A Ballad of Lovely Women (p. 116): "Pepper-flower chamber" refers to the Empress' apartments, and hence to the person who occupies them, in this case Yang Guifei, the Emperor's favorite concubine. The "kin" are her sisters, who were given the titles of the former nations of Han, Qin and Guo.

Rhinoceros horn was believed to have magical properties, in this case ostensibly as a poison detector, which gives "long-sated" an ironic twist; further, rhinoceros horn was also believed to have aphrodisiac properties, which gives yet another level of meaning to "long-sated" and connects to the sexual innuendo below.

Chief Minister Yang Guozhong arrives; second only to the Emperor in power, he was Yang Guifei's cousin (the apparent reason for his advancement) and widely hated.

Folklore held that the water-weed (frogbit) was generated by the willow-down; the word for willow, *yang*, is the same as Yang Guozhong's surname; there was a rumor that the Minister was carrying on an incestuous relationship with his cousin the Duchess of Guo; this is amplified by the mention of the bluebird, the traditional bearer of love notes. Thus, the whole poem seems satirical.

Beside Serpentine Lake (p. 117): The First Lady of Zhaoyang Palace was Lady Flying Swallow, favorite concubine and later Empress of Han Dynasty Emperor Qeng; Du Fu and other poets commonly substituted her name for that of the current Emperor's concubine Yang Guifei. This poem was composed during the occupation of Changan by An Lushan rebels. Emperor Xuanzhong and his court fled the rebel advance through Jiange Pass; at Mawei, by the Wei River, the Emperor's military escort mutinied and killed Chief Minister Yang Guozhong, the cousin of Yang Guifei, and demanded her death as well; Yang Guifei was strangled. The Emperor is "he who left" and Yang Guifei is "she who stayed"—naturally, they cannot communicate with each other. Her soul is "tainted with blood" because she was murdered and because she and her family were widely blamed for the revolution.

South is the direction of Du Fu's family; north is the location of the court in exile.

The Pitiful Young Prince (p. 119): Line 5: An allusion to the Prince of Dai's race to Changan in time to be proclaimed Emperor; successful, after running nine horses to death, he became Emperor Wen of the Han dynasty. Here, it is an ironic reference to the less-than-heroic flight of the royal court from An Lushan's rebel forces.

A *tael* is an ounce of silver.

The camels were sent by the rebel leader to carry away the loot of the capital city.

The Five Tombs were those of the Han emperors, but again, Du Fu is referring to the tombs of the previous Tang emperors.

Imprisoned . . . (p. 121): Luo Binwang was imprisoned in the year 678 for his criticism of Wu Zetian, who later became the Empress Wu. In 684, after she had deposed her son, Luo wrote an official denunciation of her and joined a rebellion led by Xu Jingye.

Inscribed at a Staging Post (p. 123): Dayu Mountains are actually in Guangdong province, more than 500 miles south of Gansu.

Sent to Left Reminder Du Fu (p. 124): Written 757–758 when Cen Shen was a Right Rectifier of Omissions in the Secretariat-Chancellery, a slightly less humble position than Du Fu's. This post was at Suzong's court in exile.

Listening to a Monk . . . (p. 126): "Green damask" was the name of the lute played by Sima Xiangru, not the one the monk actually played.

"Frost-ringing bells" were an ancient set of bells reputed to be so perfectly made that they would ring at the touch of frost settling on them. Mount Emei was the site of a number of Buddhist monasteries.

Moored at Night . . . (p. 126): West River refers to the Yangzi. Cow Island was a stopping-place for travelers on the Yangzi, located near the present-day Dangtu, Anhui. General Xie was Xie Shang (308–357). One moonlit autumn night, when he was stationed near Cow Island, Xie Shang heard someone chanting beautiful poems from a boat out on the river. He learned it was a poet named Yuan Hong. General Xie invited Yuan Hong to join him on his boat and they spent the entire night talking. Li Bai laments the lack of such a fortunate circumstance in his own life, encountering someone in power who recognizes poetic talent. Some believe this is one of his last poems.

Moonlit Night (p. 127): In the autumn of 756, Du Fu was in rebel-controlled Changan while his family was back at Fuzhou in Northern Shaanxi.

Regarding This Spring (p. 127): Composed in spring 757. Literally 10,000 taels of gold, or roughly 375 kilograms in today's measures.

Spring Vigil . . . (p. 127): Written when Du Fu had a minor position at the chancellery as a Reminder—one who is supposed to remind the Emperor of matters he might otherwise have forgotten.

Thinking of My Brothers . . . (p. 128): White Dew is the term for the two-week period beginning thirty weeks after the lunar new year.

Missing Li Bai . . . (p. 129): Composed ca. 759 at Qinzhou. Wild geese were reputed to carry messages.

A Second Farewell . . . (p. 129): Fengji is in Sichuan. Yan Wu had been promoted to a dukedom.

At the Grave of Grand Marshal Fang (p. 129): Written in 765, two years after Fang Guan's death. An influential figure in Du Fu's earlier career, Fang had been sent away from the capital to low-ranking posts in the provinces, but was recalled to Changan in September 763 to be Minister of Justice. He died on the way, at a monastery in Langzhou. He was posthumously given the rank of Defender-in-Chief. Two years later, Du Fu passed by the grave and wrote this poem, comparing Fang to Xie An (320–385), who vanquished the barbarian hordes of Fu Jian. Du Fu refers to the story of Ji Zha, who on his first meeting with the Lord of Xu noticed that the Lord admired his sword. Not finding an appropriate occasion to make him a gift of it, he resolved to present it to him on his return, but the Lord had died by the time he came back. Ji Zha hung his sword on a tree beside the grave.

Written While Traveling at Night (p. 130): Yan Wu had died in 765. Having lost his patron, Du Fu decided to leave Chengdu. He wrote this while travelling downstream.

On Yueyang Tower (p. 130): Composed in the winter of 768. The tower is the western gate tower in the city walls of Yueyang, with a fine view across Lake Dongting. Du Fu often refers to his age and infirmity in his later poems, for good reason. While in Changan during the occupation by An Lushan's rebel army, he had contracted malaria and a chronic respiratory disease; later, in Chengdu, he suffered from rheumatism, and after moving to Kuizhou he became paralyzed in his right arm, deaf in one ear, and lost all of his teeth.

Staying in the Mountains . . . (p. 131): The last two lines echo "Summons for a Recluse," one of the ancient Songs of Chu.

A View of Lake Dongting . . . (p. 134): Meng is sending Zhang Jiuling a message: appoint me to your administration. The reference to boat and oars stands for a minister's aid to his king, as in the *Shu Jing*, "Yue Ming," part one: King Wu says to Yue, his new prime minister "If I am crossing a great stream, I will use you for my boat and oars."

Line 6 refers to Confucian Analect 8:13 "When a country is well-governed, poverty and deprivation are things to be ashamed of; when a country is ill-governed, wealth and honor are things to be ashamed of." "Dangling fishing lines" refers to patrons who select their favorites for promotions and advancement.

Climbing Mount Xian . . . (p. 134): Yang Hu (221–278 CE) was a revered official under Emperor Wu of the Jin Dynasty. After his death, the people of Xiangyang built a monument to him on Mount Xian, where it became something of a tradition for people to visit and weep in his memory.

A Feast . . . (p. 135): The bluebird was said to be the messenger of Xi Wangmu, the Queen Mother of the West, an ancient goddess whose origin can be traced back to the fifteenth century BCE. She is the guardian of the peaches of immortality, and feeds them to the gods at a great banquet once every three thousand years, to enable them to stay immortal. Red Pine is one of the Divine Husbandmen, founder of agriculture and medicine.

Poem Sent to Old Friends . . . (p. 136): Donglu is a town in Zhejiang on the Fuchun River.

Written on New Year's Day (p. 139): Jia Yi was an influential official in the court of Han Dynasty Emperor Wen. He was an advocate of Confucian reforms and made some enemies who engineered his banishment. He wrote poems comparing his fate with that of Qu Yuan (See note for "Hard Road (3)," p. 112, above). Changsha became known as "The home of Qu and Jia,"

On Huai River . . . **(p. 140):** The Han River is a tributary of the Yangzi, joining it at Wuhan in Hebei Province. The Huai river runs east–west, roughly midway between the Yellow and Yangze Rivers; it traditionally marks a dividing line between north and south China; it is also a tributary of the Yangze, finally joining it at Jiangdu in Jiangsu Province.

Seeing Off Li Zhou . . . **(p. 140):** Jianye is modern Nanjing.

Happy to Meet My Cousin . . . **(p. 143):** Line 5: Literally "a thing like the great ocean" meaning a great change.

Overnight . . . **(p. 143):** Yunyang is in present-day Shaanxi Province.

Autumn Day . . . **(p. 147):** Tong Pass borders on the three provinces Shaanxi, Shanxi and Hunan. Hua Mountain, the westernmost of the Five Sacred Mountains, is in Shaanxi. Zhongtiao is another prominent mountain in Shaanxi.

Wind and Rain (p. 148): "Green Pavilions" are wine-houses or brothels.

Farewell . . . **(p. 150):** Hanyang is one of three cities now merged into modern Wuhan, the capital city of Hubei Province.

Thoughts of Antiquity . . . **(p. 151):** In 847, for his plain-spoken criticism of government policy, Ma Dai was demoted to a low-ranking post at the present-day town of Changde in Hunan, on the Yuan River near where it flows into Lake Dongting. He wrote this poem in his southern exile. A political interpretation of the female spirit of the dew mixing with the male sunlight in the first line is that the Emperor is being influenced too strongly by his ministers. The faint sun implies a weak ruler; apes crying, that people are suffering.

Thoughts on the Road to the Three Ba . . . (p. 152): Three Ba is an area in the Three Gorges.

Night Thoughts . . . (p. 154): Zhangtai was once a favorite spot for lovers to meet; it eventually became a euphemism for any pleasure house.

On the Double Ninth . . . (p. 157): During the Warring States period, the once strong state of Jin was partitioned into three, the states of Han, Zhao, and Wei, referred to as the "Three Jin."

Yin Xi was the Guardian of the Western Pass who is said to have admitted Laozi to Hangu Pass, where he produced the Dao De Jing. The reference to Tao Yuan Ming (Tao Qian) alludes to his famous poem "Drinking Wine #5":

Picking chrysanthemums at the east fence / I become aware of the South Mountain; / in clear mountain air at sunset / groups of birds are returning home. / There's a deep truth revealed in this: / try to tell it and the words are gone.

Climbing Phoenix Terrace . . . (p. 157): Phoenix Terrace was built by Emperor Wen of the Song Dynasty, near Jinling, capital of the Six Dynasties: Wu, Eastern Jin, Song, Qi, Liang, and Chen. The terrace lies south of the present-day city of Jiangning, in Jiangsu Province. The Three Peaks lie to the southeast of Jinling along the Yangzi shore. The two rivers are two branches of the Yangzi as it divides to flow around Egret Island. Li Bai wrote this after he had been dismissed from the Court in Changan. Clouds covering the sun is a stock allusion to evil advisors of the Emperor clouding his judgment or usurping his power.

Saying Farewell . . . (p. 158): Xiazhong is near Baxian in Sichuan Province. Green Maple River is near Changsha (White Emperor City).

The last line is a sly attempt to assign an official reason for an outing in the park.

After Long Rain . . . (p. 160): Line 7: A quotation from *Yu Yuan* about Yang Zhu who became very humble after he was criticized by Laozi for his arrogance.

The Chancellor of Shu (p. 161): Written in 760. The Chancellor was Zhuge Liang, who had earned a reputation for brilliance, but was living in retirement on Sleeping Dragon Hill at the time the "Three visits" were paid him by Liu Pei. Liu was a soldier who considered himself the legitimate heir to the Han Empire, and in his visits he begged Zhuge Liang's help in regaining the title. Zhuge rejected him twice, but finally agreed on the third visit, having been persuaded of Liu's sincerity and determination by his willingness to humble himself.

Welcoming a Guest (p. 161): The traveler, or guest, is his relative Cui Mingfu.

Climbing the Tower (p. 163): The Tower of the poem is the tower of the temple of the First King of Shu, in Chengdu.

Passing the Night . . . (p. 163): After five years with no employment, Du Fu had finally been given a nominal court position by Governor Yan Wu which would enable him to assume the rights and appurtenances of official rank, and thus a measure of security.

Elegies on Ancient Sites (1) (p. 164): "The world": literally the rivers and passes.

Elegies on Ancient Sites (3) . . . (p. 164): Jingmen is Jingmenshan in Hubei. The Bright Consort is Wang Zhaojun.

Elegies on Ancient Sites (4) (p. 165): The reference to feathered banners indicates that he led his army in person.

Visiting a Daoist Temple (p. 168): The Five Gateways belong to a mythical island paradise.

Sad Thoughts in Spring (p. 169): Mayi Pass is in Shanxi Province; Dragon's Mound is a desert south of the Tuanshan Mountains.

The poet adopts the familiar strategy of using events from the Han period to comment on Tang politics. In 89 CE, the Han General Dou Xian defeated the Xiongnu tribes near Mount Yan in present-day Mongolia, by pursuing them a thousand miles northward into their homeland. Perhaps Huangfu Ran is satirizing the generals of his day for their inability to stop repeated Tibetan incursions into the Tang Empire, instead signing treaties with them. This poem has also been attributed to Liu Changqing.

Climbing the Gate Tower . . . (p. 170): The four governors in the title were among a group of young officials all demoted during Wang Shuwen's brief administration in 805. The description of the river's winding course as "twisted bowels" can be read as signifying deep distress or sadness.

Thinking of the Past . . . (p. 170): West Pass Mountain is in Hubei. It is where, in the Six Dynasties period, Sun Ce defeated Huang Zu in battle.

The Patterned Lute (p. 173): This famous poem is dense with allusions. The Chinese lute, or *se*, has twenty-five strings, although it was said originally to have had fifty. However, an angry god broke it in half and ever since the number remained at twenty-five.

Master Zhuang is the philosopher Zhuangzi, who famously dreamed he was a butterfly. Waking, he didn't know whether he was a man dreaming he was a butterfly, or a butterfly dreaming he was a man.

King Wang, legendary ruler of Shu, died of shame after an illicit love affair, but was reborn as a cuckoo. One traditional name for the cuckoo, derived from its call, is *cuigui*, meaning "hurry back."

Lines 5 and 6: It was believed that pearls would only form under a full moon. There is also a legend of a mermaid whose tears turned into pearls. The Blue Mountain is famous for its jade. Jade was the name of the daughter of legendary King Wu, who died of a broken heart, but her spirit reappeared, drifting like smoke.

Untitled (p. 173): Hide the hook: a traditional game involving two teams; as the name implies, one team has to guess which member of the other team has the hook. Orchid Terrace is another name for the palace library, where Li was employed at the time.

Untitled (p. 174): The fifth watch: Dawn. The celestial peak is Peng Mountain, dwelling place of the Eight Immortals.

Untitled (p. 174): The purpose of lines three and four is obscure, but they may highlight the situations alluded to in lines five and six. The gold toad is probably an incense-burner, but why does it "bite the lock"? The jade tiger, as the poem states, is the ornamental pulley over a well.

Mistress Jia was the daughter of Jia Zhong, the Jin Dynasty prime minister. She peeped through the curtain at Secretary Han Shou, and an affair followed, only to be discovered by her father, who smelt her perfume on Han. Unusually, there was a happy ending, because they were permitted to marry.

Lady Fu was loved by Cao Zhi, celebrated poet and son of the great Han Dynasty general Cao Cao. She married Cao Zhi's brother, the first Emperor of Wei, but when she died, the Emperor gave her pillow to the poet. After a vision in which they were united, Cao Zhi wrote his famous poem "Goddess of the River Lo."

Li Shangyin is apparently using these legends to express the complications and suffering of his own passionate love affair.

At the Staging Post . . . (p. 175): The subject is Zhuge Liang, (b. 181 CE) the great military strategist of the Three Kingdoms period, who is said to have invented, among other things, the land mine and a new type of deadly crossbow. His exploits are celebrated in the *Romance of the Three Kingdoms*.

Untitled (p. 175): Penglai Mountain is the dwelling-place of the Eight Immortals of Daoist legend. The bluebird is the messenger of Xi Wangmu, Queen Mother of the West.

Untitled (p. 176): The term for "Goddess," *shennu*, is also a traditional term for a prostitute.

The Southern Ferry Dock . . . (p. 177): Lizhou is the present-day town of Guangyuan on the Jialing River in northeast Sichuan, famous for the Thousand Buddha Cliff carvings, and for being the birthplace of the Empress Wu Zetian.

Su Wu's Memorial Temple (p. 177): Su Wu (140–60 BCE) was a Han Dynasty statesman. In 100 BCE Emperor Wu sent Su as ambassador to the Xiongnu. Betrayed by his deputies, Su tried to commit suicide, but his life was saved. However, in spite of threats, he refused to surrender, even after imprisonment in a cell with no food and drink. His survival surprised his captors and he was exiled to Lake Baikai to tend sheep, where he heard news of his family's dissolution and of Emperor Wu's death. He finally returned to the Han capital, where in fact he did receive recognition and honors for his faithful service from the new Emperor.

Thinking of Each Other (p. 181): Red Sandalwood (*Adenanthera pavonina*), produces small red beadlike seeds in the fall and winter. It is also called *xiangsishu*, the "thinking of each other tree," that name echoed in the last line.

Looking at the Snow ... (p. 182): This is reputed to be Zu Yong's required poem from the Presented Scholar examination. It should have had twelve lines but he rolled up his paper and stopped after writing these four. The examination proctor asked him why he had stopped. He replied, "The idea is complete."

The Eight Formations (p. 183): The "Eight Formations" is an arrangement of sixty-four groups of large stones. Until they recently disappeared beneath the Three Gorges Reservoir, they stood in shallow water near the shore of the Yangzi River southwest of Fengjie. They are said to be the Shu general Zhuge Liang's depiction of the battle formation he would use in the decisive battle against the kingdom of Wu.

Clinbing Crane Tower (p. 184): The Crane Tower was at Hezhong, near the present-day Yongji in Shanxi, on the shores of the Yellow River. It was three stories high and offered magnificent views of the Zhongtiao Mountains and the river. The tower was later destroyed in a flood.

In the "Jade Terrace" Style (p. 186): When a woman's sash falls open spontaneously, it is understandably an omen of something good about to happen. The word for spider has the same sound as a word meaning happy. *New Songs from the Jade Terrace* was a pre-Tang poetry anthology.

River Snow (p. 186): This quatrain is Liu Zongyuan's most famous poem. Its simple language and evocative imagery have made it one of the best-known poems in Chinese. Since he wrote it after he was demoted to the far south, where snow never falls, some also see in it an ironic comment on his own official career: banished, alone, and wasting his talent far from the Court.

Invitation to Liu Nineteen (p. 187): Literally Liu the Nineteenth. The "ants" are small impurities that float on the surface of the unfiltered newly-brewed rice wine.

Master He's Tune (p. 187): She sings a song about Master He, or He Man Zi, a singer whose last poem before he was executed became a favorite among the palace women.

Crossing the Han River (p. 188): This poem is also attributed to Song Zhiwen.

Spring Grievance (p. 189): The Liao River is in present-day Liaoning, where her husband was serving with the army.

At the Frontier (2) (p. 191): The reference is to a story about the Han general Li Guang. Hunting at night, he thought he saw a tiger when the wind parted the grass. He shot an arrow at it. In the morning, he found his arrow sunk deep into a stone. Angry that it wasn't a tiger, he shot at the stone again, but this time his futile arrow bounced off.

A Southern Tune (p. 192): Qutang is one of the Three Gorges of the Yangzi River.

Spring in the Palace (p. 195): The Weiyang was a Han palace, built as an audience hall. It was rebuilt in the Tang to accommodate the Emperor's concubines and favorites. The Pingyang Princess, concerned that the Han Emperor Wu had gone so long without a wife, organized a party, inviting ten of the most beautiful women she knew. The Emperor came, but found none of them to his liking. However, when the princess ordered dancers to perform, he immediately chose one of the dancers as his new concubine, later to become the Empress.

Liangzhou (p. 195): Liangzhou is in northern Gansu.

Seeing Meng Haoran Off . . . (p. 195): The Yellow Crane Tower was on a mountain west of the present-day city of Wuhan, with a spectacular view eastward over the Yangzi River valley.

Leaving Early . . . (p. 196): White Emperor City is a small group of old temples and buildings on a peninsula in the Yangzi River near the town of Fengjie. Now, it lies beneath the water of the Three Gorges Reservoir. This poem celebrates Li Bai's return from exile; at White Emperor City he received news of the Emperor's pardon.

Meeting Li Guinian (p. 196): Li Guinian was a famous singer, a favorite of the Bright Emperor and his court in the period before the An Lushan rebellion. This was Du Fu's last quatrain, written shortly before his death at Changsha in 770.

On the West Bank . . . (p. 197): This quatrain is an excellent example of the allusive layer in Tang poetry. The thirteenth-century poet Xie Fangde chose this poem to begin a primer for young scholars on writing and interpreting poetry. He wrote:

> The shaded grass growing by the side of the gorge is the gentleman in the wilderness, who has to find his enjoyment by the side of the gorge. The yellow orioles calling in the deep woods are villains in office, whose cunning words are like the river's rapid current. The water in the gorge naturally flows fast, but swollen by the spring rains, we know it will become a torrent. In the same way, we know the nation's hardships have increased. Since the flow becomes more urgent at evening, we know there is danger to the nation and confusion among those at Court as their season in power is drawing to its end. In the same way, we know the evening sun is growing dim and will not brighten again before it sets. "At this deserted ferry one must get the boat across alone," means he is in a vast wilderness, on a deserted riverbank and yet he has the talent to help the world cross the figurative river at this moment of its hesitation, just as he is able to manage the actual river crossing without help from anyone. It would be an unusual ruler who, reading this, would not make use of him.

Grievance of One on a Campaign (p. 198): The grave belongs to Wang Zhaojun. The places named were in the northwestern frontier region, the present-day area of Inner Mongolia, Gansu and Xinjiang.

Climbing the Wall . . . (p. 199): Huile is near Wuzhong in Ningxia. Shouxiang is on the north bank of the Yellow River, near Wujiahe, at the northernmost point of its great bend through Inner Mongolia.

Crow Robe Alley (p. 199): Redbird Bridge and Crow Robe Alley in Jinling boasted the mansions of the leading families of the Eastern Jin Dynasty. More than four hundred years later, what remains of their grandeur?

Given to a Woman in the Palace (p. 201): Swallows sleep in pairs, but she is alone. If only releasing her from her own servitude were as easy as setting free the moth trapped in her room.

On the Terrace of Gathered Spirits (2) (p. 201): The Consort-of-State Guo was Yang Guifei's youngest sister. She was executed with her sister at the Ma Wei Post Station.

About to Leave for Wuxing (p. 202): Written in the autumn of 850, before Du Mu went out to Huzhou as Prefect. Wuxing is another name for Huzhou.

Sent to Administrative Assistant Han Chuo . . . (p. 203): In Du Mu's time, Yangzhou was one of the finest cities in China, a prized post for civil servants. Han Chuo had become his friend during his tour of duty there between 833 and 835. Du Mu wrote this quatrain some time after his transfer away from Yangzhou, presumably to a post that lacked much of what made Yangzhou so pleasant.

Given in Parting (2) (p. 204): Du Mu met Zhang Haohao in 827 when he was posted to the Jiangxi Surveillance Commission at Hongzhou. She was a thirteen-year-old singing girl among the retainers of the Commissioner. The following year, the Commissioner was transferred, and Zhang Haohao went with him to his new post. Du Mu met her again five years later in Luoyang and wrote these quatrains as a parting gift.

Night Rain, Sent North (p. 205): Ba Mountains are in the eastern part of Sichuan. Li wrote this to his wife while posted to Zizhou as an Administrative Assistant on the staff of the Regional Military Commissioner there.

Message to Secretary Linghu (p. 205): This poem was written for Linghu Tao, the son of Linghu Chu. He was Li Shangyin's influential friend at the Imperial Court, but he refused to use his position to advance Li's career. The sickness is identified in the poem as *xiangru*, the symptoms of which are similar to those of diabetes. However, since some scholars called to serve the state sometimes pleaded illness, this may have been Li's way of showing his indifference to officialdom.

The Sui Palace (p. 206): This refers to Emperor Yang of the Sui Dynasty, who ruled from 605 to 617. He is often lampooned for his debauchery, corruption, and extravagance. He spent most of his rule away from his capital, on long expensive trips to the provinces. Shortly after his death, the Sui Dynasty fell.

Jasper Lake (p. 206): King Mu of the Zhou dynasty is famous in legend for mounting expeditions to find out what lay beyond the borders of his kingdom. After a long journey to the west, he met the Queen Mother of the West in the Kunlun Mountains at her palace near Jasper Lake. After a brief and passionate visit, he left to return to his kingdom, but promised to come back to her in three years. On a later journey, he saw many of his people frozen to death after a freak storm. He composed the "Yellow Bamboo Song" as an elegy to them and resolved never to leave his kingdom again. The traditional date of his death is 946 BCE.

Chang E (p. 206): Chang E stole the elixir of eternal life and fled to the moon. Now, the goddess of the moon, she lives forever, cold and alone.

Master Jia (p. 207): Jia Yi (201–169 BCE) was a minister at the court of the Han Emperor Wen. After banishing him, the Emperor recalled him for a consultation, not about how to improve his government, but to ask about ghosts and spirits. The story is famous as an example of a wasted opportunity. This poem has also been attributed to Du Mu.

233

Mawei Slope (p. 207): Another poem about the death of Yang Guifei. (See the note to "The Song of Endless Sorrow," p. 92). The last Emperor of the Chen Dynasty (557–589) hid with his two favorite concubines in a well at his palace when the rebels invaded and destroyed his capital. The Bright Emperor, in the end, lost both his Consort and his throne.

Already Cool (p. 208): Dragon beard grass is a rush that grows along riverbanks, used for weaving mats. This poem is considered to be Han Wo's masterpiece.

A Picture of Jinling (p. 208): Wei describes the place where Emperor Wu of the Liang Dynasty starved himself to death in 550.

Anonymous Poem (p. 209): The cuckoo calls "Hurry back" (See note for "The Patterned Lute," p. 173).

Wei City Song (p. 210): Wei City was another name for the town of Xianyang, on the northern bank of the Wei River about fifteen miles northwest of Changan. The Yang Pass is southwest of Dunhuang. This farewell poem was written for a friend off on a journey to Anxi, the present-day Kucha in Xinjiang. This poem became immensely popular during the Tang period, especially chanting or singing it at farewell parties.

Autumn Night (p. 210): This poem is sometimes attributed to Wang Ya.

Grievance in the Ever-Faithful Palace (p. 210): This quotes from Han-era poems by Lady of Handsome Fairness Ban, a discarded concubine of the Cheng Emperor (ruled 32–6 BCE). After she lost his favor, she was sent to live in the Ever-Faithful Palace. Among her poems of that period was one complaining that although she swept dust from her rooms, it was futile because no one ever came to see her. In another, she compared herself to a beautiful fan—prized and always at hand during the summer but laid aside and forgotten once autumn came.

Crossing the Frontier (p. 211): The Flying General was Li Guang, of the Han Dynasty, claimed by the Tang royal house as their ancestor.

The Shadow Mountains are in the central part of present-day Inner Mongolia.

Crossing the Border (p. 211): Nor does the concern of their Emperor reach them, fighting on the distant western frontier.

Clear and Bright Tunes (1–3) (p. 211–212): These three quatrains were written impromptu at a flower-viewing party where the Emperor and Precious Consort Yang were in attendance. They were written to music and performed by the famous singer Lu Guinian. Li Bai could even turn bald flattery into something memorable.

Biographies of the Poets

BAI JUYI was born in 772. His family was originally from Taiyuanfu, but by the time he was born, they had moved to Xiagui in Huazhou. He was a prodigy, composing poems by age six. He passed the examination for Presented Scholar in 800 and the more difficult Preeminent Talent examination in 803, along with his close friend Yuan Zhen. His first appointment was Editor in the Palace Library. In 806, he and Yuan Zhen passed yet another special examination, this time for the prestigious degree Understanding and Knowledge Both Excellent. In 807, for his "One Hundred New Yuefu Poems," the Xianxong Emperor named him a Hanlin Academician. Over the next few years, through his outspoken prose and satirical poetry, he earned the enmity of some powerful men at court. His mother died in 811 and he left office for the official mourning period, after which he received appointment as Left Grand Master Admonisher in the Secretariat of the Heir-Apparent. In 815, he wrote a memorial criticizing the government for not acting more decisively in bringing Wu Yuanheng's murderers to justice. For this rashness, not waiting for the official machinery to conduct an inquiry, he was demoted to Jiangzhou as Vice-Prefect. Three years later, he moved to Zhongzhou as Prefect. In 820, the Muzong Emperor took the throne and recalled Bai Juyi to Court. He became Director of the Bureau of Receptions in the Ministry of Rites and Participant in the Drafting of Proclamations. In 821, he was promoted to Secretariat Drafter. After a year there, during which he proctored the re-examination of the 820 Presented Scholar candidates, he requested an assignment in the provinces to distance himself from the controversy. He became Prefect of Hangzhou, where he served for two years. Following a brief assignment in Luoyang, he was appointed Prefect of Suzhou in 825. In the fall of 826, he became ill and returned to Luoyang. A year later, he received the prestige title Director of the Palace Library, and in 828, added that of Vice-Minister of Justice. In 829, he chose to return to Luoyang for good, serving in the ceremonial posts of Junior Mentor of the Heir-Apparent and later Governor of Henan until he became ill again in 833. During the next few years, he spent much time with his friends Liu Yuxi and Pei Du. In 842, the Wuzong Emperor wanted to make Bai Juyi a Grand Councilor, but factional rivalries prevented it: Li Deyu blocked the appointment on the pretext of Bai Juyi's age (70) and poor health. His career at an end, Bai Juyi formally retired in 842, with the courtesy rank of Minister of Justice. He died in 846. His poetry was extremely popular during his lifetime, both among the literati and among the common people. His surviving poetry fills almost one tenth of the pages of the *Complete Tang Poems*.

CEN SHEN was born in 715, a native of Jiangling in Jingzhou. He came from a family with a tradition of civil service. A great-grandfather, great uncle and uncle were all Grand Councilors and his father was Prefect of Jinzhou. Cen Shen passed the examination for Presented Scholar in 744. His first assignment was as Adjutant in the Military Service Section of the Left Inner Guard Command. In 749, he was transferred from his post at the Capital as Administrative Supervisor of the Right Awesome Guards, to the headquarters staff of Gao Xianzhi. For two years, Gao was Regional Military Commissioner of Anxi. Cen Shen was back in Changan from 751 until 754, where he was able to spend much of his free time with his friends Chu Guangxi, Gao Shi, and Du Fu. In 754, he was appointed a Case Reviewer in the Court of Judicial Review and Acting Investigative Censor, attached to the headquarters of Feng Changqing, the Regional Military Commissioner of Beiting, sometimes called Dzungaria, on the far northwest frontier. During the An Lushan rebellion, he joined the Bright Emperor's court-in-exile in 757 as a Right Rectifier of Omissions. Two years later, he was promoted to Imperial Diarist in the Secretariat-Chancellery, then transferred to be Prefect of Guozhou. In 761, he became a Palace Censor on detached duty as the Administrative Assistant to the Regional Military Commissioner of Guanxi. After two years there, he returned to the Capital as a Vice-Director of the Bureau of Sacrifice in the Ministry of Rites, but he soon moved to the Ministry of Personnel as Director of the Bureau of Merit Titles. In 765, he was appointed Prefect of Jiazhou, but due to a rebellion there, had to turn back while still en route. In 766, he moved to the Ministry of War as Director of the Bureau of Operations and concurrently Palace Censor. In that post, he went out to Chengdu on the staff of the Regional Military Commissioner of Jiannan, Du Hongzhe. That allowed Cen Shen to take up his appointment as Prefect of Jiazhou in 767. A year or so later, he retired and traveled eastwards as far as Chengdu, where he died in 770. Like his friend and contemporary Gao Shi, he has been most famous for his poems about war.

CHANG JIAN was a native of Changan. He passed the examination for Presented Scholar in 727, in the same class as Wang Changling. During the Tianbao period (742–756), he served as a District Defender in Xuyi. He did not achieve much success in his career, and because of his disappointment, he lost interest in his duties. After a period of traveling, wine, and music, he resigned and lived the rest of his life as a private citizen. During his lifetime, his poetry was admired almost as much as that of his contemporaries Wang Wei and Meng Haoran.

CHEN TAO was from northern China. He came to Changan during the Taizhong Period (847–860) to study for the examinations but failed them repeatedly. He traveled home by way of some famous scenic locations, but finally settled as a recluse on West Mountain in Hongzhou. When he died, his friends Guan Xiu, Cao Song, Fang Gan and Du Xunhe all wrote elegies for him.

CHEN ZIANG was born in 661, a native of Shehong in Zizhou. As a youth, he was more interested in studying swordsmanship than the Classics, and only began preparing for the Presented Scholar examination at the age of eighteen. He failed in 682, then passed in 684. He attracted the notice of Wu Zetian, whose influence helped him receive an appointment as a Proofreader in the Palace Library. In 693, he rose to Right Reminder in the Secretariat. Around 699, Chen Ziang's father died and he left government service to return home to Sichuan for the required mourning period. He was also frustrated at the Empress having made so little use of his advice. In 702, the local magistrate of his home district, acting under instructions from Wu Sansi, the Empress Wu's cousin, threw him into prison, where he died. Many later Tang poets regarded him as an exemplar of their own careers: the virtuous minister, ill-used by his ruler, who writes allegorical poetry to express his criticisms.

CUI HAO was a native of Bianzhou. Recognized as a child prodigy, he passed the examination for Presented Scholar in 723. After a period of travel in southern China, he was appointed an Investigating Censor in 730. By 742, he was Assistant Minister of the Court of the Imperial Stud. That year, he became Vice Director of the Bureau of Merit Titles in the Ministry of Personnel. Later, he wrote poems lampooning the abuses of the Imperial concubine Yang Guifei and her kinsman Yang Guozhong, for which they transferred him to the frontier. He died in 754. Li Bai passed by the Yellow Crane Temple and saw a poem written there by Cui Hao, and though invited to, he declined to add one of his own.

CUI SHU was a native of Bailing, but by the time of his birth, his family had moved to Songzhou. Though born to a poor family of common origin, he studied diligently. He passed the examination for Presented Scholar in 738 and was appointed District Defender at Henei. His examination poem soon became famous, but he died the following year. Fifteen poems survived.

CUI TU was born around 850, a native of Tonglu in Wuzhou. He first took the examinations in 881, at the temporary Court in Chengdu, where the Xizong Emperor had fled the Huang Chao rebels. He failed that time, but finally passed in 888. Nothing is known of his later life.

DAI SHULUN was born in 732, a native of Jintan in Runzhou. As a young man, he was well regarded for his writing. Around 767, he took up his first official position, as Capital Liaison for the Transport Commissioner. A few years later, while on duty at Kuizhou, he persuaded a local rebel, the General Yang Zilin, to surrender. For this, he received a promotion to Probationary Investigating Censor and Magistrate of Dongyang. In 783, he moved to Hongzhou to join the headquarters staff of the Surveillance Commissioner of Jiangxi. After a few years out of office, he was appointed Prefect of Rongzhou in 787. He became ill in the summer of 789 and requested permission to enter a Daoist temple. He died within a few months. He was posthumously named a Presented Scholar in 800.

MISS DU QIU: This poem is sometimes attributed to a Miss Du Qiu, although the editors of the *Complete Tang Poems* listed it as anonymous. The attribution to Du Qiu comes from a mention of her in the works of Du Mu, and has become generally accepted in recent times. Du Qiu may have been the wife of an imperial clansman who lived in the latter part of the eighth century.

Du Fu was born in 712. He was a native of the capital, but his actual birthplace is unknown. His father Du Xian, and his grandfather Du Shenyan, both held official rank. In his early years, Du Fu traveled widely. By the middle 730s, he was in Changan, where he failed the examination for Presented Scholar at his first attempt, probably in 735. He spent most of the next ten years in Changan. While living in the Capital, he met and became friends with Li Bai. He failed the Presented Scholar examination a second time in 747, the year Li Linfu contrived to have every candidate fail. From 751 to 754, Du Fu periodically sent essays to the Bright Emperor, hoping for an appointment. All he received from the Emperor were compliments. In 755, aged forty-two, he was finally appointed to a minor post in the Right Guards Grand Command. The An Lushan rebellion was just beginning. He became a refugee, unable to take up the post. After the Suzong Emperor took the throne in 756, Du Fu was appointed a Left Reminder in the Secretariat-Chancellery at the court in exile. In 758, caught up in a change of faction at court, he was demoted to Administrator in the Personnel Evaluation Section in Huazhou. In 759, worried that the continuing rebellion endangered his family, he left that post. They traveled westward to Tonggu in Qinzhou, where they lived in difficult conditions. In 761, he again moved his family, this time to Chengdu, where he received an appointment as an Aide in Yan Wu's headquarters. After Yan Wu died in 766, Du Fu lost his patron. He shifted his residence to the Yangzi river town of Kuizhou, later renamed Fengjie and recently destroyed to make way for the Three Gorges Reservoir. In 768, he was again on the move with his family, moving gradually down the Yangzi River. In 770, he fell ill and died near Tanzhou, present-day Changsha in Hunan. Du Fu is indisputably China's greatest poet.

Du Mu: Cousin of the famous Du Fu, Du Mu was born in 803, a native of Changan. He passed the examination for Presented Scholar in 828, as well as the special examination for men designated Worthy and Excellent, Straightforward and Upright. He was first appointed an Editor in the Institute for the Advancement of Literature. After a tour as an Inspector of Militia in Jiangnan, he joined the headquarters staff of the Surveillance Commissioner of Jiangxi at Hongzhou. In 833, Niu Sengru promoted him to be his Chief Secretary when Niu was Regional

Military Commissioner of Huainan, stationed at Yangzhou. Though not a main instigator, he was associated with the Niu faction in the Niu-Li factional struggle. In 835, he went to Luoyang as Investigating Censor in the Luoyang Branch Office. Two years later, he was back in the field at Xuanzhou as Assistant Military Training Commissioner on the staff of the Surveillance Commissioner of Xuanshe. In 838, he was recalled to Changan as a Left Rectifier of Omissions and Senior Compiler in the Historiography Institute. After serving as Vice-Director of the Bureau of Review in the Ministry of Justice and of the Catering Bureau in the Ministry of Rites, he was appointed Prefect of Huangzhou in 842. He transferred as Prefect to Chizhou in 844, and Muzhou in 846. In 848, he was recalled to the Capital as Vice Director of the Bureau of Merit Titles, and once again Senior Compiler in the Historiography Institute. Two years later, he was again in the provinces as Prefect of Huzhou, but returned to Changan in 851 as Director of the Bureau of Evaluations in the Ministry of Personnel and Participant in the Drafting of Proclamations. His final post, in 852, was Secretariat Drafter. He died that year.

Du Shenyan was born around 645, a native of Gongxian in Henanfu. He passed the examination for Presented Scholar in 670. He was appointed an Editorial Director in the Palace Library. He later attained the position of Vice Director of the Catering Bureau, from which post he was banished in 705 to the distant town of Fengzhou (near the present-day city of Hanoi) for his relationship with Zhang Yizhi and the Empress Wu's faction. After his recall in 706, he served as a Recorder in the Directorate of Education and Auxiliary Academician in the Institute for the Cultivation of Literature. He died in 708. Du Shenyan was Du Fu's grandfather.

Du Xunhe was born in 846, a native of Shidai in Chizhou. One story says that he was Du Mu's son by a concubine, conceived while Du Mu was Prefect at Chizou. Whatever his pedigree, as a young man he was unsuccessful in the examinations. After failing, he traveled across much of South China to avoid the Huang Chao rebellion and lived as a recluse for fifteen years. He finally passed the examination for Presented Scholar at the age of forty-six, in 891, placing first that year. He took no post and returned home, the government being in disarray because of unrest and rebellions. When Tian Jun was Garrison Commander of Xuanzhou, Du Xunhe served on his staff. In that post he became acquainted with Zhu Wen, who later founded the Posterior Liang Dynasty after he deposed and executed last Tang Emperor, Zhaozong, Zhu Wen admired Du Xunhe's talent and appointed him to offices in his breakaway Court: first Hanlin Academician, and later Vice Director of the Bureau of Receptions in the Ministry of Rites and Participant in the Drafting of Proclamations. Du Xunhe died in 904.

GAO SHI was probably born around 700, a native of Bohai. As a child, he lost his father, a former Prefect of Shaozhou. He grew up in poverty. Gao Shi arrived in Changan around 719 to look for an official appointment, but had no success. He headed to the northeastern frontier and saw combat service against the Turks. He returned to Changan in 735 for a special examination, which he failed. After several years traveling with his friends, including Wang Zhihuan, Wang Changling, and Zhang Xu, he settled down in Xiangzhou. A few years later, in 747, he spent some time with Du Fu and Li Bai. He sat for another special examination in 749, which he passed. He was appointed District Defender in Fengqiu. He soon went out to the northwestern frontier as a Section Adjutant in the Left Courageous Guards, serving under the famous general Geshu Han. After several years back at Court as a Grand Master of Remonstrance, he went to the field again as Regional Military Commissioner of Huainan at Yangzhou. Despite his success in this post, he was slandered by a rival and relieved of his post. He spent the next few years in Luoyang on the staff of the Heir-Apparent. Following a tour as Prefect of Shuzhou beginning in 760, he was again posted in 763 as a Regional Military Commissioner, this time of Jiannan at Chengdu, front line in the wars with the Tibetans. He was not as successful in this post. In 764, he was relieved and recalled to the Capital as one of the Daizong Emperor's Policy Advisers in the Secretariat-Chancellery and ennobled as Marquis of Bohai. He died in 765. His frontier poetry is often compared to that of Cen Shen.

GU KUANG was born around 727, a native of Suzhou. He passed the examination for Presented Scholar in 757, the same year as Yan Wei. He served first in the Salt Monopoly Bureau. From 771 until 774, he traveled in Huzhou, exchanging poems with the monk Jiaoran and others. Later, while traveling, he met Liu Hun and Li Bi. In 780, he was appointed an Administrative Assistant to the Regional Military Commissioner at Zanhuang. In the early 780s, Liu Hun attained a high office in the Capital. Gu followed him to Changan, where Liu secured for him an appointment as a Rectifier in the Court of Judicial Review. In 787, with Li Bi's help, he was appointed Editor, and in 788, Assistant Editorial Director in the Palace Library. Both Li Bi and Liu Hun died in 789. Shortly afterwards, Gu Kuang was accused of satirizing the dominant court faction in his poetry. He was demoted to Raozhou as a Revenue Manager. In 793, he retired and went to live at the Daoist center on Mount Mao. From 794 until the early 800s he traveled throughout central China. He was still alive in 806 and probably lived well into his eighties.

HAN HONG was a native of Nanyang in Huaizhou. He passed the examination for Presented Scholar in 754 but waited at Changan until 761 for his first posting, to the headquarters staff of Xi Yi, then Regional Military Commissioner of Zizhou and Qingzhou. In 765, Xi Yi was relieved by one of his deputies and returned to Changan. Han Hong returned with him. For the next ten years he lived there as a private citizen, spending time with his friends Lu Lun and Qian Qi among many others. In 774, he again joined the headquarters staff of the Xuanwu Regional Military Commissioner at Bianzhou. He served successive Commissioners there until 780. That year, the Dezong Emperor, admiring his poem on the Cold Food Day, personally appointed him Director of the Bureau of Equipment in the Ministry of War, and Participant in the Drafting of Proclamations. He rose to be a Secretariat Drafter before his death, probably in the middle 780s. Han Hong was one of the "Ten Geniuses of the Dali Period."

HAN WO was born in 842, a native of the capital, Changan. The famous poet Li Shangyin was his brother-in-law and had recognized Han Wo's poetic skill while he was still a child. He passed the examination for Presented Scholar in 889, the same year as Wu Rong. He was initially appointed a Hanlin Academician and Left Reminder in the Secretariat-Chancellery, then a Bureau Director in the Ministry of Personnel. By 901, he was a Secretariat Drafter and Recipient of Edicts. He was very close to the Zhaozong Emperor (reigned 889–905), and a strong and vocal opponent of the eunuchs who were in control of the Court. The Emperor, hoping to weaken the eunuchs, repeatedly asked Han Wo to become a Grand Councilor and head the administration. Each time, he refused. In 903, his rival Zhu Quanzhong had him demoted to a provincial post in Sichuan. In 905, he was restored to his rank and position but did not return to the Capital to take them up, fearing it was a pretext to have him assassinated. He remained in the south as a private citizen and probably died around 914.

HAN YU was born in 768, a native of Heyang. He was orphaned at age three and raised by his elder brother's widow. He passed the examination for Presented Scholar in 792, the same year as Wang Ya. His first post was in 796, as a Judge on the staff of the Regional Military Commissioner for Xuanwu at Bianzhou. Around 796, he was at Xuzhou as a staff officer at the Wuning Regional Military Commission. By 802, he was in Changan as Erudite of the School of the Four Gates. In 803, he was promoted to Investigating Censor. He was soon demoted to District Magistrate at Yangshan for submitting a memorial urging a reduction of taxes. From 806 until 811, he was at Luoyang as Erudite of the National University in the Luoyang Branch Office, and later Vice-Director of the Criminal Administration Bureau. In 811, he returned to Changan as Vice-Director of the Bureau of Operations in the Ministry of War. For the next six years, he served in several Bureau-level appointments, punctuated by occasional demotions for his outspokenness. In 817, he joined the staff of the Grand Councilor Pei Du as his Adjutant when Pei was quelling the rebellion in Huaixi. For his service to Pei Du, he was appointed Vice Minister of Justice. In 819, for a memorial criticizing the court's extravagant planned ceremonies for receiving a bone of the Buddha, he was demoted again, this time to be Prefect of Chaozhou in what is now rural Guangdong Province. The following year, the Muzong Emperor recalled him to be Chancellor of the Directorate of Education. Later, he was promoted to Metropolitan Vice-Governor, then Vice-Minister of War, and finally Vice-Minister of Personnel. He died in 825. Han Yu was a fine poet, but is better known as a leader of the Guwen (Ancient Style Writing) Movement, seeking to restore the vigorous prose style of the classical period.

HE ZHIZHANG was born in 659, a native of Yongxing in Yuezhou. He was well-known as a young man for his poetry. He passed the examination for

Presented Scholar in 695 and was appointed an Erudite of the School of the Four Gates and later Erudite of the Court of Imperial Sacrifices. He was a protégé of Zhang Yue. Beginning in 723, Zhang's influence helped him secure a series of appointments including Academician in the Academy of Scholarly Worthies, Vice-Minister of Rites, and Director of the Palace Library. He retired in 744 to return home and became a Daoist priest, but died the same year. During his life, he befriended the younger poets Li Bai and Du Fu. Fond of drinking, he is one of the "Eight Immortals of the Wine Cup." He was also renowned as a calligrapher.

HUANGFU RAN was born in 717, a native of Danyang in Runzhou. By the time of his birth, the family had moved to Anding. He learned to read at an early age, and when he was only fifteen, Zhang Jiuling praised his writing. He passed first as Principal Graduate in the 756 examination for Presented Scholar, the same year as Lang Shiyuan. His first appointment was as a District Defender in Wuxi. After two years there, he resigned and traveled for a while in southeast China. Afterwards, he returned to service as an Adjutant in the Left Imperial Insignia Guard. In 764, when Wang Jin was Regional Military Commissioner of Henan at Luoyang, he appointed Huangfu Ran his secretary. In 767, he returned to the Capital as a Left Reminder and then Left Rectifier of Omissions in the Secretariat-Chancellery. He died in 770. Among his close friends were Liu Changqing, whom he knew from childhood, and Yan Wei.

JIA DAO was born in 779, a native of Fanyang in Youzhou. As a young man, he became a Buddhist monk and took the name Wu Ben, meaning "rootless." In 810, he renounced the monkhood and followed Han Yu, an early admirer of his poetry, from Luoyang back to Changan. Jia Dao took the examinations many times, but despite the sponsorship of Han Yu and the support of other prominent men of the day, he never passed as a Presented Scholar. He spent many years in Changan, but he also traveled widely during later periods of his life. In 837, he received an appointment as Assistant Magistrate at Changjiang in Suizhou. Three years later, he was transferred to nearby Puzhou as Administrator of the Granaries Section. In 843, he died before he could assume new duties in the Revenue Section at Puzhou. Jia Dao was a master of the five-word quatrain, regarded as the equal of Meng Jiao. The great Song dynasty poet Su Shi said of them that he disliked "the coldness of Meng Jiao and the hunger of Jia Dao."

THE MONK JIAORAN: Jiaoran was a Buddhist monk. He was born around 720, a native of Changcheng in Huzhou. His original surname was Xie and he claimed to be the tenth generation descendant of the poet Xie Lingyun (385–443). Around 742, he failed the examination for Presented Scholar. Bitterly disappointed, he took refuge in the Changan Temple at Jiangning in Runzhou, where he became a monk and took the name Jiaoran. In the early 750s, he traveled throughout China, spending time at many important temples and monasteries. He settled in Huzhou and became a leading figure in lower Yangzi literary circles. He had many influential friends and exchanged poems with an impressive list of the poets of the day, including Yan Zhenqing, Gu Kuang, Huangfu Ran, Liu Zhongyong, Yang Ning, Li Jiayou, Yan Wei, Ling Che, Zhu Fang, Wei Yingwu, Li Duan, Quan Deyu, Bao Ji and Meng Jiao. Meng Jiao in particular was greatly influenced by Jiaoran. Even more than his fame as a poet was his influence as a literary critic. Jiaoran died sometime before 793, the year his collected works were compiled by Imperial decree.

JIN CHANGXU: This is the only surviving poem by Jin Changxu, a native of Yuhang. Nothing else is known of him.

LI BAI was born in 701. His family was originally from Central Asia and like many in that frontier region, of mixed Turk and Chinese blood. He was probably born at Suiye, also called by its Turkish name Tokmak, the present-day Bishkek, capital of Kyrgyzstan. Around 705, his father moved the family to Sichuan, where Li Bai grew up. Another version of his early years says he was born in Sichuan. As a youth, he read the Classics extensively, but also studied swordsmanship. His genius attracted the attention of Su Ting, who predicted he would have a brilliant official career. Following a long period of travel beginning in 724, he arrived in the capital around 730 to look for a sponsor. Although he became part of the circle of the Yuzhen Princess, and He Zhizhang admired his writing, nothing came of it. He left the Capital in 732, continuing his travels. By 742, he was back in Changan, at the invitation of the Yuzhen Princess. He received an appointment to the Hanlin Academy, ironically among those offices that did not require success in the examinations. Despite some close contact with the Bright Emperor, by 744 his penchant for appearing at court drunk, and other offenses, had earned him a discharge. He spent the next several years traveling and staying with his friends, among them the poets Du Fu and Gao Shi. Later, he traveled in the frontier area. When the An Lushan rebellion broke out in 755, Li Bai took a minor post on the staff of Prince Yong, one of the Imperial Princes then wrangling to be Heir-Apparent. When the brief rebellion of his patron was defeated in 757, Li Bai found himself in prison. He was almost executed. After his release, beginning in 759, he continued to travel until his death in 762, hoping all the time to find a way back to a position in the central government. With Du Fu, Li Bai is considered one of China's two greatest poets. He is also remembered as one of the "Eight Immortals of the Wine Cup."

LI DUAN was a native of Zhaozhou. The poet Li Jiayou was his uncle. He passed the examination for Presented Scholar in 770 and was appointed an Editor in the Palace Library. After service in Hangzhou in the early 780s, he retired and lived as a private citizen near Hengshan. He died a few years later, sometime before 786. Li Duan was one of the "Ten Geniuses of the Dali Period" and was a friend of many of the other "Geniuses," among them Lu Lun, Han Hong, Qian Qi, Sikong Shu, and Geng Wei.

LI LONGJI was the first Xuanzong Emperor, also called Ming Huang, the Bright or Brilliant Emperor. He was born in 685, the third son of the Ruizong Emperor. In 710, the Zhongzong Emperor suddenly died and the Empress Wei took control of the palace, placing her young son Li Chongmao on the throne. Within a few weeks, Li Longji led troops who killed her and her followers, then placed his father on the throne. For this, he became a Grand Councilor, holding the rank of Director of the Palace Cooperating with the Rank Three Officials of the Secretariat. Soon he added Heir-Apparent to those titles. The following year he became Regent. He succeeded his father on the throne in 712. His long reign saw the Tang Empire reach the height of its brilliance, and after 740, the beginning of its decline. In his later years, he fell under the influence of the powerful eunuch faction at court, aided by the family of his notorious concubine, Yang Guifei. The Sogdian general An Lushan's rebels captured the capital in the summer of 756, and the Emperor and his advisors fled toward Chengdu. About thirty miles west of Changan, at the Mawei post station, his army commanders refused to continue unless he allowed them to put Yang Guifei to death. The Emperor agreed. Before his party arrived in Chengdu, his third son usurped the throne. After the new Suzong Emperor's forces recaptured the two Capitals in 757, the former Emperor returned to Changan, where he lived in retirement until his death in 762.

LI QI was a native of Yingyang in Yingzhou. He passed the examination for Presented Scholar in 735, in the same class as Li Hua and Du Fu. He was posted as District Defender in Xinxiang, where he served for many years. He later retired and returned home to Dengfeng where he studied alchemy in an attempt to prolong his life with drugs and medicines. Li was a good friend of the poets Gao Shi, Wang Wei and Wang Changling and exchanged poems with them on many occasions. He died sometime after 750.

LI SHANGYIN was probably born in 813, a native of Henei in Huaizhou. While still in his teens, his poetry attracted the attention of Linghu Chu, a leader of the Niu faction at court, then serving as Regional Military Commissioner of Tianping, in Shandong. Linghu gave Li Shangyin a junior post in his headquarters. In 833, he went to Changan for the Presented Scholar examinations. He failed that year, and again in 835, the year of the Sweet Dew Incident. He finally passed as a Presented Scholar in 837, in no small part due to the influence of Linghu Tao, Linghu Chu's son, then serving as a Rectifier of Omissions. Li served again briefly on Linghu Chu's staff, but Linghu Chu died in 838. That year, Li Shangyin joined the staff of Wang Maoyuan, then Regional Military Commissioner of Jingyuan at Jingzhou, as a Secretary. Wang was an influential member of the Li faction. Li Shangyin soon married one of Wang's daughters. The traditional histories blame Li's failure to attain much success in his later career to his marriage across the fault line between the Niu and Li factions. Linghu Tao was particularly resentful, accusing Li Shangyin of having "forgotten my family's favors and put advantage ahead of loyalty." In 839, Li Shangyin received the low-ranking sinecure post of Editor in the Palace Library, but was soon sent out as District Defender of a small district in Henan. In 842, Li Shangyin rejoined his father-in-law's staff. That year, he passed the prestigious examination for Preeminent Talent, which guaranteed him an appointment. However, he only received another low-ranking sinecure post, this time as a Proofreader in the Palace Library. For the next sixteen years, Li Shangyin moved from one minor office to the next, sometimes with long periods of unemployment between. After his wife died in 851, he embraced Buddhism. He died out of office in 858, in Zhengzhou. Much of Li Shangyin's poetry is densely allusive and difficult to understand. Nonetheless, he is considered to be one of the greatest poets of the Late Tang.

LI YI was born in 748, a native of Guzang in Longxi. He passed the examination for Presented Scholar in 768. He spent the first ten years of his career as District Defender, and later Assistant Magistrate at Zhengxian in Huazhou. In 780, he went to the northern frontier for a year as a headquarters staff officer. In 784, he passed a Special Recruitment examination and was appointed an Attendant Censor. From 788 until 796, he again served as a staff officer, this time at the Binning Regional Military Commission at Binzhou, northwest of Changan. After a year off, in 797 he transferred to the headquarters at Youzhou, where he served until 806. Around 806 or 807, he came to Court as Vice-Director of the Criminal Administration Bureau in the Ministry of Justice. By 809, he was a Secretariat Drafter, and the following year became Vice-Governor of Henan. The Xianzong Emperor admired his poetry and appointed him Vice-Director of the Palace Library and an Academician in the Institute for Advancement of Literature. He was briefly relieved of his duties in 813 because of a satirical poem. For the next seven years, he moved through a series of offices including Mentor to the Heir-Apparent, Director of the Palace Library, and Supervisor of the Academy of Scholarly Worthies. His career was aided by his association with the Niu faction in the Niu-Li factional struggle. His highest office was Minister of Rites. He died in 827. His poetry on military themes was well regarded by his peers and afterward. Li Yi also acquired the reputation in later generations for being a cruel and unfeeling husband, as immortalized in the ninth-century "Story of Huo Xiaoyu."

LIU CHANGQING was probably born around 710, a native of Xuan-
zhou, but his family had been living at Changan for many years when
he was born. As a young man, he lived at Songshan while studying for
the Presented Scholar examinations, but failed several times. He only
passed much later, around 755, following some years as a student at the
National University. After waiting out the period of the An Lushan rebel-
lion, he finally took up his first post, District Defender at Changzhou,
in 757, aged in his late forties. Within a year, he was acting Magistrate
at Haiyan, but was demoted for some offense to be District Defender
in remote Nanba, where he served until 761. After a period of travel in
southern China, he returned to the Capital in 763 and probably served as
a Palace Censor until the late 760s. By 769, he was Vice-Director of the
Bureau of Sacrifice in the Ministry of Rites, on detached duty as Capital
Liaison Representative for the Yangzhou-based Transport Commissioner.
In that post, while on liaison duty at Ezhou with the Eyue Surveillance
Commission in 775, the Surveillance Commissioner impeached him for
insubordination. He was demoted to be Vice-Magistrate of Wuzhou. The
Dezong emperor ascended the throne in 779. Liu, by then perhaps seventy
years old, was rehabilitated and appointed Prefect of Suizhou. In 782,
when the Regional Military Commissioner of Huaixi began a rebellion
against the central government, Liu resigned his office and retired to a
village near Yangzhou, where he died, probably in 790.

LIU FANGPING was a native of Luoyang. He came from a long line of
civil servants. His father was an Investigation Commissioner in the
south and Liu Fangping grew up in a wealthy household. He failed the
examination for Presented Scholar in 750. He served for a while in a
military headquarters, but was keenly disappointed at his examination
failure, and soon resigned. He lived the rest of his life as a recluse in the
mountainous area of the Ru and Ying Rivers in what is now northern
Anhui. He was a good friend of the poets Yuan Jie, Huangfu Ran, and
Li Qi. Twenty-six poems survived.

LIU SHENXU was a native of Xinwu in Hongzhou, the present-day
Fengxin in Jiangxi. He probably passed the examination for Presented
Scholar during the Kaiyuan period (713–742), and later the more difficult
examination for Erudite Literatus. He served for a while as an Editor in

the Institute for the Advancement of Literature, but the rest of his life is a mystery. Among his friends were Wang Changling, Meng Haoran and Gao Shi. After Meng Haoran died in 740, Liu Shenxu led an effort to gather Meng's surviving works for publication.

Liu Yuxi was born in 772. He was a native of Luoyang, but his family had moved to Jiaxing in Suzhou by the time he was born. As a young man, he studied poetry with the monks Jiaoran and Lingche. He passed the examination for Presented Scholar in 793, the same year as Liu Zongyuan. He later graduated as Erudite Literatus. His first post, in 795, was as an Editing Clerk in the Secretariat of the Heir-Apparent. By 800, he was at Yangzhou as Private Secretary to the Regional Military Commissioner of Huainan. After a year as Assistant Magistrate at Weinan, he entered the central administration in 803 as an Investigating Censor. In early 805, when Wang Shuwen became a Grand Councilor, he brought Liu into the Imperial Palace as one of his closest advisers. He received the merit post of Vice Director of the State Farm Bureau and Supervisor of the Revenue Section of the Salt Monopoly Bureau. When Wang Shuwen lost power later that same year, Liu was demoted to be Prefect of Lianzhou. While en route to that post, he was further demoted to Deputy Prefect of Langzhou, in Hunan. Disheartened at this setback, he wrote many bitter and satirical poems. In 814, after nine years in the provinces, he was recalled to the capital. He was awaiting an appointment when he wrote his famous poem about seeing the flowers at the Xuandu Temple, in which he ridiculed those who had come to power in the ten years since Wang Shuwen had fallen. This resulted in another transfer away from the Capital, this time to Bozhou. Pei Du interceded with the Xianzong Emperor to have Liu's post changed to the less-remote Lianzhou. In 821, he moved to Kuizhou as Prefect, and in 824, to Hezhou. In 826, he resigned and returned home to Luoyang. In 827, he was appointed Vice-Director of the Bureau of Receptions in the Luoyang Branch Office of the Ministry of Rites. In 828, he was once again summoned to Changan to take up the post of Director of the Bureau of Receptions. It was then he wrote his poem, "Once Again Visiting the Xuandu Temple." Before long, he became an Academician in the Academy of Scholarly Worthies. In 831, he went out as Prefect of Suzhou, later serving as Prefect of Ruzhou and Tongzhou. In each of these Prefectures, he was an exemplary administrator, doing much to improve the lot of the people. In 836, suffering from an ailment of the legs, he received a sinecure appointment back home in Luoyang, as Advisor to the Heir-Apparent and Acting Minister of Rites. He died in 842. In his youth Liu Yuxi had a close relationship with Liu Zongyuan, and during his later years he also spent a few years with Bai Juyi and Pei Du at the latter's retirement home at Luoyang.

LIU ZHONGYONG: Liu Dan, better known by his courtesy name Liu Zhongyong, was a native of Yuxiang in Puzhou. He was an elder clansman of the famous writer Liu Zongyuan, and a close friend of the poet Li Duan. In 774, he was living in Huzhou, where he and his friends, including the calligrapher Yan Zhenqing and the monk Jiaoran, compiled a book of their poems. Later, he moved to Hongzhou, where he died.

LIU ZONGYUAN was born in 773, a native of Hedong in Puzhou. He passed the examination for Presented Scholar in 793, and in 796 the prestigious examination for Erudite Literatus. He was appointed a Proofreader in the Academy of Scholarly Worthies. In 803, he went to Lantian as District Defender. In 804, he returned to Changan as a Probationary Investigating Censor. At court, he joined the group of men around Wang Shuwen and became Vice-Director of the Bureau of Ceremonials in the Ministry of Rites. When Wang Shuwen fell from power in the autumn of 805, Liu Zongyuan was demoted to Revenue Manager in Yongzhou. After nine years there, he was recalled in 815 to the capital, but—like his friend Liu Yuxi—almost immediately sent out again, this time as Prefect of remote and rural Liuzhou. He died at his post in 819. More revered as a prose writer, he nevertheless produced some memorable poems.

LU LUN was born around 735, a native of Puzhou. Beginning in 767, he failed the examination for Presented Scholar several times. In 771, the Grand Councilor Yuan Zai appointed him District Defender at Wenxiang and later Magistrate at Mixian. Around 773, Wang Jin appointed him Academician in the Academy of Scholarly Worthies and an Editor in the Palace Library. During this time, he became friends with Qian Qi and Li Duan. When Yuan Zai and Wang Jin fell from power in 777, Lu Lun was dismissed and left the capital for a post in the provinces. By 784, he was serving as Administrative Assistant to the Vice-Marshal of the Fengtian Mobile Brigade. When his patron was promoted to Regional Military Commissioner of Hezhong, Lu Lun moved with him. In early 798, the Dezong Emperor inquired about Lu Lun's whereabouts, and had him transferred back to Changan so they could exchange poems. The Emperor appointed him Director of the Census Bureau in the Ministry of Revenue, where he served until his death a year or so later. Lu Lun was one of the key members of the group of poets known as the "Ten Geniuses of the Dali Period."

LUO BINWANG was born around 627, a native of Yiniao in Wuzhou. He was recognized as an excellent poet as early as age seven. Some time after 670, Luo came to Changan and took the post of Vice-Director for Ceremonials in the Court of Imperial Sacrifice. Because of some offence, he was transferred to military duties on the Western frontier. After that tour, he was posted to Chengdu. There, he met and become friends with Lu Zhaolin. Returning to the Changan area, he served as Assistant Magistrate at Wugong, Mingtang, and finally Changan itself. He was an early opponent of Wu Zetian's power at court, and spent some time in prison for his outspoken criticisms. At the time of the Gaozong Emperor's death in 684, Luo had reached the position of Attendant Censor. That year, he joined the rebellion of Xu Jingye in support of the legitimate heir to the throne. He probably died in the defeat of their army by forces under the control of Empress Wu, though one account says he escaped and became a Buddhist monk. Luo Binwang was one of the "Four Masters" of early Tang poetry.

MA DAI: After earlier failing the examinations, Ma Dai passed as a *jinshi* in 844, the same year as Xiang Si and Zhao Gu. Early in the Dazhong period (847–860), he served at Taiyuan as Chief Secretary in the Private Secretariat of the Hedong Regional Military Commissioner. For some outspoken, and apparently unwelcome advice, he was demoted to District Defender of Longyang in Langzhou, the present-day town of Changde in Hunan. He later rose to become Erudite of the National University. Among his close friends were other poets of the period, including Yao He, Jia Dao, and Yin Yaofan.

MENG HAORAN was born in 689, a native of Xiangyang in Xiangzhou. As a young man, he lived in seclusion on Deer Gate Mountain near Xiangyang, writing and studying for the examinations. In 728, for the first of many times, he went to Changan to take the examination for Presented Scholar. He failed the next sitting, in 739, and several more times as he grew older. Between 730 and 733, he traveled in Southeastern China, spending time with friends, including Cui Guofu. In 733, he returned to Changan, but had no success in attracting attention at Court. In 737, his friend Zhang Jiuling was demoted to a provincial post in Jingzhou, and appointed Meng Haoran to his local administration. In 739, he resigned because of illness and returned home to Xiangyang. The next year, Wang Changling passed through Xiangyang and found Meng Haoran gravely ill. He died a few days later, aged 52. During his life, he was a friend of Li Bai, Du Fu and Wang Wei.

MENG JIAO was born in 751, a native of Wukang in Huzhou. In his younger years, he lived as a private citizen at Songshan, where he became acquainted with Han Yu. After failures in 792 and 793, he left Changan and traveled widely for a few years before he finally returned to pass the examination for Presented Scholar in 796, aged forty-six, the same year as Cui Hu. After waiting four years for an official post, he was appointed District Defender at Liyang. He did not apply himself to his duties, spending so much time writing poetry and wandering the countryside that the Magistrate frequently complained to his superiors. By 804, Meng Jiao had had enough; he resigned on the pretext of needing to care for his aging mother. He went to live in Luoyang. During the next two years, he counted Han Yu and Zhang Ji among his friends. Around 806, when Zheng Yuqing was Governor of Henan, he appointed Meng Jiao Administrative Assistant to the Water and Land Transport Commissioner. Three years later, Meng Jiao left office to observe the official mourning period for his mother. In 814, Zheng Yuqing went out to garrison Xingyuanfu. Zheng appointed Meng Jiao as a Counselor in his headquarters, but Meng became ill and died on the way to take up the post. He never attained any high position in the government and this disappointed him all his life. He was so poor at his death there was not enough money for a funeral.

PEI DI: In his early years, Pei Di lived with Wang Wei and other friends at South Mountain, near Changan. There, he and Wang exchanged many poems. Later, when Wang Wei acquired his country state at Felloe Creek, Pei Di often stayed there with him. In 760, he served on the staff of Wang Jin, Wang Wei's younger brother, when the latter was Prefect of Shuzhou. At Suzhou, he made friends with poets such as Du Fu and Li Qi. After Wang Wei's death, he continued his official career, eventually attaining the high office of Director of the Department of State Affairs.

QIAN QI was born around 710, a native of Wuxing in Huzhou. He passed the examination for Presented Scholar in 751 and was first appointed an Editor in the Palace Library, then in 759 District Defender at Lantian. At Lantian, he became friends with Wang Wei, then near the end of his life. They exchanged many poems. After Wang's death in 761, some saw Qian Qi as his poetic successor. In 764, he returned to the Capital. During the Dali Period (766–779), he served as Vice-Director of the Bureau of Sacrifices in the Ministry of Rites, and Director of the Bureau of Merit Titles in the Ministry of Personnel. During this period, he became friends with Lu Lun. In 780, he moved to the Bureau of Evaluations as Vice-Director and probably died around 782. Qian Qi was known during his lifetime as one of the "Ten Geniuses of the Dali Period," considered the equal of Lang Shiyuan at composing quatrains. The late Tang poet Qian Xu was his descendant.

QIN TAOYU was a native of Hunan. Because his father served as Commanding General of the Left Army, Qin Taoyu was well-known at the Palace. He failed the Presented Scholar examination several times, presumably because he offended someone. When the Huang Chao rebels captured Changan in 880, he fled to Sichuan with the Xizong Emperor, who appointed him Vice-Minister of Works and Supervisor of the Salt Monopoly Commission. In 883, he received the Presented Scholar degree by special proclamation.

QIU WEI was probably born around 690, a native of Jiaxing in Suzhou. He repeatedly failed the examinations for Presented Scholar as a young man, then returned home to continue his studies in seclusion. He finally passed the examination in 743, by then in his fifties, in the same class as Zheng Wei. He served as Director of the Bureau of Receptions in the Ministry of Rites and later Director of the Bureau of Merit Titles in the Ministry of Personnel. His highest position was Right Mentor to the Heir-Apparent, when he was over eighty, and still living with his aged mother. He lived to be ninety-six, dying sometime after 785. Among his closest friends were Wang Wei and Liu Changqing.

QIWU QIAN was a native of Nankang in Qianzhou, now part of Jiangxi. He passed the examination for Presented Scholar in 727. While nominally appointed as a local police official, he served as an Auxiliary Academician in the Academy of Scholarly Worthies. By the end of the Kaiyuan era (713–742), he held the sinecure rank of Editor in the Palace Library. In 742, he left the civil service and returned to his home district. Around 753, he returned to service as a Right Reminder and later Editorial Director in the Secretariat-Chancellery. His later career and the date of his death are unknown. Among his friends were Wang Wei, Meng Haoran, Li Qi, Gao Shi, and Chu Guangxi.

QUAN DEYU was born in 761, a native of Lueyang in Tianshui. He was a child prodigy, allegedly composing his first poem at the age of four and writing well-regarded scholarly essays before he was fifteen. In 780, he was appointed an Editor in the Palace Library. He served as Erudite of the Chamberlain for Ceremonials during the Zhenyuan period (785–805), rising to be Vice Minister of Rites. By 806, he was Vice Minister of War and later Chief Minister of the Court of Imperial Sacrifices. In 810, he became Minister of Rites and jointly Manager of Affairs with the Secretariat-Chancellery, one of the highest posts in the civil administration. In 816, he went out to become Regional Military Commissioner of the Shannan and Shanxi areas, where he became ill. He died en route home to the capital in 818.

SHEN QUANQI was born around 656, a native of Neihuang in Xiangzhou. He passed the examination for Presented Scholar in 675, the same year as Song Zhiwen. He was appointed a Chief Musician in the Court of Imperial Sacrifice and became associated with the circle of Wu Zetian's favorite, Zhang Yizhi. By 699, he was a Secretarial Receptionist. In 701, he became Vice Director of the Bureau of Evaluations, and Supervising

Secretary the following year. In 705, the Zhongzong Emperor resumed the throne and banished him to Huanzhou in present-day Vietnam, the southernmost prefecture in the Empire, because of his association with Zhang Yizhi and the Empress Wu's faction. The following year, he was pardoned and his career resumed with appointments as Imperial Diarist and concurrently Academician in the Institute for the Advancement of Literature, later Secretariat Drafter, and finally Junior Supervisor of the Household of the Heir Apparent. He died around 713. His poetry was famous during his lifetime and he was often paired with Song Zhiwen in style and skill.

SIKONG SHU was born around 720, a native of Guangping in Gongzhou. He passed the examination for Presented Scholar in 767. Between 772 and 773, he served as a Reminder in the Secretariat-Chancellery. During this period, he became friends with Qian Qi and Lu Lun. A few years later, he was demoted to Assistant Magistrate at Changlin, where he reported to Wei Xiang. Later still, he served in the military headquarters of Wei Gao in Chengdu, and then back in Changan as Acting Director of the Bureau of Waterways in the Ministry of Works. Sikong Shu was one of the "Ten Geniuses of the Dali Period."

SONG ZHIWEN was born around 656, a native of Xihe in Fenzhou. He passed the examination for Presented Scholar in 675. In 689, along with Yang Jiong, he served as an Auxiliary in the Institute for the Study of the Polite Arts (a school for the palace women). After service as an Adjutant in Luozhou, he returned to the Capital as Aide to the Supervisor of the Directorate for Imperial Manufactories and Auxiliary Left Grand Master of the Palace Corral. Here, he became a protégé of Zhang Yizhi, the Empress Wu Zetian's favorite. When the Zhongzong Emperor resumed the throne from the Empress Wu in 705, he executed Zhang Yizhi and demoted Song Zhiwen to a minor post in the Provinces. The following spring, Song returned secretly to the capital and betrayed a friend's plot against the Empress Wu's nephew. The Empress rewarded him with the post of Assistant Magistrate in Honglu, but soon recalled him to the Capital and promoted him to be a Vice-Director of the Ministry of Revenue and Auxiliary Academician in the Institute for the Cultivation of Literature. In 708, be became Vice-Director of the Bureau of Merit

Titles in the Ministry of Personnel, and the following year, Director. In these posts, he ingratiated himself with two of the Imperial Princesses and took bribes from candidates for ranks and appointments administered by his office. Soon exposed, he was again demoted to the low rank of Aide in Yuezhou. The Ruizong Emperor ascended the throne in 710, and further banished Song Zhiwen to Qinzhou, a small coastal town near the present-day Vietnam border. There, around 712, the newly enthroned Bright Emperor graciously allowed him to commit suicide in lieu of execution.

WANG BO was born in 650, a native of Longmen in Jiangzhou. At the time of his birth, his family had moved to Taiyuan. He was a grandnephew of Wang Ji and was a child prodigy, publishing his first scholarly work at age nine, a lengthy correction to the annotations in the standard edition of the *Han History*. He passed the Presented Scholar examination at a very early age and served as Senior Compiler in the Princely Establishment of one of the Gaozong Emperor's sons. In 669, after displeasing the Emperor with a satirical essay about cockfighting, he was dismissed and fled to Shu, the eastern part of present-day Sichuan. After two years there, he was recalled to the civil service and served as Adjutant in Guozhou. There, in 674, he was again accused of serious offenses and sentenced to death. After being pardoned in a general amnesty, he accidentally drowned while en route to Annan, the northern part of present-day Vietnam, around 676. His father had been banished there because of his son's disgrace. Wang Bo was one of the "Four Masters" of early Tang poetry. These poems were all written during his period of exile in Sichuan.

WANG CHANGLING was born around 690, a native of Changan. He passed the examination for Presented Scholar in 727, in the same class as Chang Jian, and was appointed an Editor in the Palace Library. In 734, he passed the difficult examination for Erudite Literatus and was appointed District Defender at Sishui. In 739, he was demoted for some offense to an even lower-ranking post in the south. A year later, he returned to Changan and stayed with Meng Haoran. That winter, he was sent out as an Aide at Jiangning. During the An Lushan rebellion, he was a refugee in the provinces. In 756, he was convicted of a crime and a local magistrate executed him. During his life, he had been a friend and correspondent of Wang Wei, Wang Zhihuan, Li Bai, Gao Shi, Cen Shen and others. He is considered to be a master of the seven-word quatrain.

WANG JIAN was born around 766, a native of Yingchuan in Yingzhou. Around 780 he went to Heshan in Qizhou to study for the examinations, where he met and became close friends with his fellow-student Zhang Ji. Beginning around 785, and for the next twenty years, he served as a staff officer in several military headquarters on the frontiers. Some time after in 813, he moved to Weinan as District Defender. There, he met a eunuch named Wang Shouzhang, and through him became familiar with the lives of palace women. This resulted in his famous sequence of quatrains, "One Hundred Palace Lyrics." From Weinan, he moved to Changan as an Aide in the Court of the Imperial Treasury. By 828, he was an Aide to the Court of Imperial Sacrifices. That year, he transferred to Shanzhou as an Assistant to the Prefect, but soon retired and returned to Changan, where he died some time between 830 and 835.

WANG WAN was a native of Luoyang. He passed the examination for Presented Scholar in 712 and was appointed Assistant Magistrate at Rongyang. Beginning in 718, he spent four years as member of a team of scholars engaged in the collection and publication of a complete catalog of the Imperial Library. In 722, he was appointed District Defender at Luoyang. Around 730, he was at the Imperial Court, but nothing is known of his life afterwards.

WANG WEI was probably born in 701, the same year as Li Bai. His family's native place was Qixian in Taiyuanfu, but he was probably born at Hedong in Puzhou. A child prodigy in both poetry and painting, he passed the examination for Presented Scholar in 721. His first post was Assistant Director of the Imperial Music Service, but he was soon demoted back to his home prefecture as an Administrator in the Granaries Section after a subordinate committed some lapse of manners. In 735, Zhang Jiuling, then Chief Minister, recalled Wang Wei to the capital as a Left Reminder. In 737, he was promoted to Investigating Censor. After a tour of duty as an Administrative Assistant to the Regional Military Commissioner of Hexi at Liangzhou, he returned to the central government in 740 as a Palace Censor and Director of the Bureau of Military Appointments in the Ministry of War. In 742, he moved to the Secretariat-Chancellery as a Right Reminder and later transferred to the Censorate as a Supervising Censor. In 746, he returned to the Ministry of War, first as Vice-Director and later Director of the Bureau of Provisions. His mother died in 750 and he left office to begin the official mourning period. He spent most of the next two years at his villa near Felloe Creek (Wangchuan) with his close friend Pei Di. It was during this period that they composed the sequence of forty quatrains called the "Felloe Creek Collection." In 752, after the mourning period for his mother ended, he returned to the Ministry of War as a Bureau Director until 755, then moved to the Secretariat-Chancellery as a Supervising Secretary. The An Lushan rebels captured Wang Wei when they took Changan in 756. They moved him to Luoyang and placed him under house arrest in the Bodhi Temple, then forced him to serve briefly in the rebel administration. Imperial forces retook Luoyang the next year. Wang Wei was indicted and imprisoned for having served the rebels. The Suzong Emperor pardoned him after hearing a poem he wrote while under arrest that put his loyalty beyond question. Early in 758 he was appointed an Academician in the Academy of Scholarly Worthies and Right Mentor of the Heir-Apparent. In 760, the year before his death, he attained his highest official rank, Right Vice-Director in the Department of State Affairs. Near the end of his life, Wang Wei became an adherent of the Chan sect of Buddhism and frequently took leave of his duties for meditation. Wang Wei was an expert musician and an excellent painter. In poetry, his contemporaries considered him the equal of Meng Haoran.

WANG ZHIHUAN was born in 688, a native of Jinyang in Taiyuanfu. Because his father was a District Magistrate, Wang Zhihuan entered the civil service by means of his father's Protection Privilege. His first post was Assistant Magistrate at Hengshui in Jizhou, but because of some false accusation, he soon resigned. After that, he traveled widely, gaining fame as a swordsman. Around 732, he spent some time traveling with Gao Shi. Late in life, he served as District Defender of Wenan and his fairness in this post earned him wide renown. He died there in 742. Wang Zhihuan was famous as a poet during his lifetime and was acquainted with Wang Changling and Cui Guofu. Only six poems survived.

WEI YINGWU was born around 737, a native of Changan. In 751, he became one of the Bright Emperor's bodyguards. When the Emperor was deposed in 756, Wei Yingwu began studying for the official examinations. He entered the National University in 758. After passing the examinations for Presented Scholar, he was posted to Luoyang around 765 as assistant to the Magistrate there. In Luoyang, he was impeached for dealing too severely with a disorderly soldier. He left the civil service and returned to Changan the next year. He lived there privately until 774, when he accepted a post in the Metropolitan Personnel Evaluation Section. Next, in 778, he was given a transfer away from the capital as a District Magistrate, but did not take up his post. He resigned on grounds of illness and returned to live in a temple west of the Capital. In 781, he was appointed Vice Director of the Bureau of Review in the Department of State Affairs. In 783, he went to Chuzhou as prefect, moving to Jiangzhou in 785. He was recalled to the Capital in 788 as Left Vice-Director of the Department of State Affairs. But, because of the plotting of some jealous rivals, after only a year he was sent away from the Capital yet again. This time he was appointed Prefect of Suzhou. He served three years and then retired to live in the Yongding Temple in Suzhou. He fell ill and died not long afterwards, probably in late 792.

WEI ZHUANG was born in 836, a native of Changan. He was a fourth-generation descendant of Wei Yingwu. He failed the examinations for Presented Scholar a number of times, and gave up his studies to travel for more than ten years. He finally passed in 894, when he was almost sixty. He was appointed an Editor in the Palace Library. In 900, he published a large anthology of Tang poetry. That year, as Left Rectifier of Omissions, he also submitted his famous memorial urging that several distinguished poets, among them Liu Jia, Li Qunyu, Fang Gan, Huangfu Song, and Lu Guimeng, be posthumously awarded the title Presented Scholar. In 901, he went to Sichuan, where the Regional Military Commissioner Wang Jian made him Chief Secretary at his headquarters. When Wang Jian proclaimed himself Emperor of the new breakaway Former Shu Dynasty, he appointed Wei Zhuang Vice-Minister of Personnel and concurrently Manager of Affairs. As a Grand Councilor, he served at the head of the Shu civil administration. He died in 910, having spent much of his life fleeing rebellions in a generation of disorder, the last great poet of the Tang.

WEN TINGYUN was born around 812, a native of Taiyuanfu. In the early part of the of the Taizhong era (847–860) he repeatedly failed the examination for Presented Scholar. He took a minor post as an Inspector on the staff of Xu Shang, the Garrison Commander at Xiangyang. When Xu came to the central administration, he appointed Wen Tingyun an Instructor in the Directorate of Education. When Xu Shang left office, Wen Tingyun was demoted to District Defender at Suixian. In 866, he was back in Changan, again as an Instructor in the Directorate of Education. He died around 870. Wen Tingyun had the reputation of being rash and his satire often offended those in power. During his last period in Changan, he was one of the circle of poets close to the woman poet Yu Xuanji.

XU HUN was born around 791, a native of Danyang. Although a descendant of high-ranking officials, he grew up in a poor family and his health was poor. As a young man, he traveled widely across China. He passed the examination for Presented Scholar in 832. He served as a District Magistrate, but resigned on grounds of illness. Later he returned to serve as an Investigating Censor, but once again had to resign due to ill health. After recovering his health, he again returned to the Civil Service as Vice-Prefect of Runzhou. He later served as Vice-Director of the Bureau of Forestry and Crafts in the Luoyang Branch office. He died in the late 850s while serving as Prefect of Yingzhou.

XUE FENG was born around 806, a native of Hedong in Puzhou, the present-day Yongji in Shanxi. He passed the examinations for Presented Scholar in 841 and was appointed an Editor in the Palace Library, a poorly-paid sinecure post. In 850, his patron, Cui Xuan, became a Grand Councilor and appointed Xue Feng a Supervising Censor on detached service in Luoyang. In that office, he offended a powerful court faction with some satirical poems and was demoted to Prefect of Bazhou, in the frontier area of present-day Sichuan. In 860, he was promoted to Administrator of Chengdu and concurrently Prefect of two adjacent prefectures, Fengzhou and Jinzhou. In 867, he was recalled to the Capital at Changan as Vice-Minister of the Court of Imperial Sacrifice. He died around 876. His poetry was well-regarded during his lifetime. Ninety of his poems survive.

YUAN JIE was born in 719, a native of Lushan in Ruzhou. He was a descendant of the non-Chinese Xianpi Toba clan, who were the Emperors of the Northern Wei Dynasty (424–535). They adopted the Chinese surname Yuan in the fifth century. Yuan Jie passed the examination for Presented Scholar in 754, but fled south with his family during the An Lushan rebellion. In 759, he returned to the Capital, where the Chancellor of the National University recommended him to the Suzong Emperor. As a result, he received a post in the Imperial Insignia Guard, and later that year, became Vice-Director of the Bureau of Waterways in the Ministry of Works. A year later, in 760, he went to Jiangling as Administrative Assistant to Lü Yin, the Regional Military Commissioner of Jingnan. Lü Yin died the following year, and Yuan Jie handled matters there until Lü's replacement arrived. For that service, he was appointed an Editorial Director in the Palace Library. In 763, he was posted to Daozhou as Prefect. Because of a local rebellion, he did not arrive there until 764. Somehow, he had earned the hatred of the powerful Grand Councilor Yuan Zai, who forced him to resign once more. He was restored to that post in 766, and in 768 transferred to Rongzhou as Prefect. In 769, he received the titles General of the Left Insignia Guard and Vice Censor-in-Chief. In 772, he was recalled to the Capital, but fell ill and died on the way, aged 54.

ZHANG BI repeatedly failed the examination for Presented Scholar during the Zhengyuan period (785–805). He died sometime after 816. Zhang Bi admired Li Bai and called himself Zhang Taibai in the same way Li Bai had called himself Li Taibai. Meng Jiao was an admirer of Zhang Bi's poetry.

ZHANG HU was a native of Qinghe in Beizhou. He was probably born around 792. He first lived in Suzhou and later went to Changan. During the first half of the ninth century, he was famous as a poet. Even so, he never passed the examinations for Presented Scholar. He served in a series of minor posts until he was recommended at court by Linghu Chu, with the support of Bai Juyi and Du Mu, all supporters of the Niu faction. Yuan Zhen blocked his appointment, so he left the capital disappointed, his official career ended by the Niu-Li factional rivalry. Late in life, he lived near Danyang in a mountain cottage, where he died around 853.

ZHANG JI (1) was born in 768, a native of Suzhou, but he grew up at Wujiang in Hezhou. There, in 796, he met Meng Jiao. Meng helped him obtain an appointment to the staff of the Xuanwu Regional Military Commissioner at Bianzhou where Meng Jiao and Han Yu were then stationed. With their support, Zhang Ji went to Changan and passed the examination for Presented Scholar in 798. He returned to Hezhou and did not take an official post because he was in mourning. In 806, he was appointed Great Supplicator in the Court of Imperial Sacrifices. He served there for ten years without a further promotion. During this time, he suffered from an eye ailment, and lost much of his sight. In 816, he became an Instructor in the Directorate of Education. During this time, he counted among his friends such eminent men as Han Yu, Bai Juyi, Yuan Zhen, Liu Yuxi and Pei Du. He later served as Director of the Bureau of Waterways and Irrigation in the Ministry of Works from 822 to 824. He left this post to spend time with Han Yu, who was near death. He became Director of Studies in the Directorate of Education in 827. He died around 830.

ZHANG JI (2) was a native of Xiangzhou. He passed the examination for Presented Scholar in 753 and first served in a regional military head-quarters. In 756, he fled the Capital to avoid the An Lushan rebels, and spent time in Hangzhou and Suzhou. In 767, he returned to Changan as a Censor. By 769, he was Acting Vice-Director of the Bureau of Sacrifices on detached duty in Hongzhou as Administrative Assistant to the Transport Commissioner. He died there around 779.

ZHANG JIULING was born in 678, a native of Qujiang in Shaozhou. He passed the examination for Presented Scholar in 703. In 708, he was appointed an Editor in the Palace Library. From 712 to 716, he was a Left Reminder on the staff of Li Longji, later the Bright Emperor. He rose rapidly. In 720, he became Vice-Minister of Rites. By 723, he was Vice Director of the Secretariat and jointly Manager of Affairs, effectively the second most powerful man in the government. From 727 until 731 he served in the provinces. Under the Bright Emperor, he served as Director of the Secretariat beginning in 735. Zhang Jiuling mistrusted the Sogdian general An Lushan and recommended his execution as a precaution against future rebellion. The Bright Emperor refused. For his outspokenness, his rival Li Linfu impeached Zhang Jiuling. In 737, he was demoted to Aide in Jingzhou. In the latter years of his life, he was a patron of Wang Wei and Meng Haoran. Zhang Jiuling died in 740. More than twenty years later, after An Lushan's disastrous rebellion was finally quelled, the Bright Emperor posthumously restored Zhang Jiuling's ranks and endowed pensions for his surviving family.

ZHANG QIAO was a native of Chizhou. After years of study at Mount Jiuhua, near Wuxi, he passed the examination for Presented Scholar in 871. Although he had some influential friends, he did not receive an appointment. After the Huang Chao rebellion broke out, he returned to Mount Jiuhua with some friends, including Zheng Gu, and lived the rest of his life there, studying and writing.

ZHANG XU was born around 675, a native of Suzhou. His first post was District Defender in Changshu. He later served as Administrator of the Imperial Insignia. He was a famous calligrapher, frequently doing his best work when drunk, and was called Madman Zhang for his unconventional behavior. Among his calligraphy students was the poet and monk Jing Yun. He was a friend of Li Qi, Gao Shi, and Li Bai—his fellow member of the "Eight Immortals of the Wine Cup." Zhang Xu died around 750. Only six poems survived.

ZHENG TIAN was born in 825, a native of Xingyang. In 842, he passed both the examination for Presented Scholar and the much more difficult examination for Preeminent Talent. He served first as a Judge on the staff of a Regional Military Commission, and later was appointed District Defender at Weinan and Auxiliary in the Historiography Office. Before long, his father, an influential member of the Li faction at Court, was demoted to Guizhou. Zheng Tian went with him. He later served in various non-official posts in the Taiyuan area. In 864, he was called to Court as a Bureau Vice-Director in the Ministry of Justice. Within five years, he had risen to be a Hanlin Academician Recipient of Edicts, Bureau Director in the Ministry of Revenue and Participant in the Drafting of Proclamations. Under the Xizong Emperor, he was promoted to Right Policy Advisor in the Secretariat-Chancellery, then Vice-Minister of Personnel. In 875, he became Vice-Minister of War and a Grand

Councilor. That was the year the Huang Chao rebellion began. For the next five years, debate raged at Court about the best way to deal with the rebels. In 876, he was sent to the field as Regional Military Commissioner of Fengxiang. Because of his success in that post against Huang Chao's forces, he was reappointed a Grand Councilor in 877. He was a strong opponent of Gao Pian in the court debates about how to defeat the rebels. The following year, he was again dismissed. In 880, after writing a memorial to the Xizong Emperor in his own blood, he was reappointed a Grand Councilor and Commander of the Joint Expeditionary Force. His forces had some success against Huang Chao. In 881, he was again relieved from his command and returned to Chengdu where the Xizong Emperor had fled when Huang Chao captured Changan the previous year. After a year as Acting Vice-Director of the Department of State Affairs, he received the largely ceremonial post of Grand Guardian of the Heir-Apparent. He died in 883. Sixteen poems survived, of which this is the most famous, the best-known Tang quatrain on the death of Yang Guifei.

ZHU QINGYU was born around 800, a native of Yuezhou. His official name was Zhu Kejiu, but he is usually known by his courtesy name Qingyu. When he first came to Changan for the examinations, he met Zhang Ji, who admired his work and promoted his career. He passed the examination for Presented Scholar in 826 and was appointed an Editor in the Palace Library. He later abandoned his official career and traveled in the border regions. Among his friends in Changan were Zhang Ji and Jia Dao.

ZU YONG was a native of Luoyang. He passed the examination for Presented Scholar in 724, but did not receive an official appointment. After waiting in the capital for a year, he returned home and spent the rest of his life as a private citizen. He was a close friend of Wang Wei.

Translators' Biographies

GEOFFREY WATERS received a PhD in Classic Chinese from Indiana University and worked most of his life in international banking. He died in 2007. His other books of translation include *Broken Willow: The Complete Poems of Yu Xuanji*, *White Crane: Love Songs of the Sixth Dalai Lama*, and *Three Elegies of Ch'u*.

MICHAEL FARMAN is a retired Electronics Engineer. Early in his career he studied Mandarin at the School of Oriental and African Studies, London University, but began translating Chinese classical and ancient poetry comparatively late in life. His translations have since appeared frequently in literary and translation journals and several anthologies. His chapbook *Clouds and Rain* was published by Pipers' Ash in 2003. As an active member of ALTA, he has organized and contributed to conference panels and workshops and also published articles and book reviews in *Translation Review*.

Professor DAVID LUNDE earned his B.A. from Knox College and an M.F.A. from the U. of Iowa Writers' Workshop. He taught English and directed the creative writing program at SUNY-Fredonia for 34 years. He has published eight books of poetry and two books of Chinese poetry in translation, *Breaking the Willow* and *The Carving of Insects*, the collected poems of the 20th-century poet Bian Zhilin, co-translated with Mary M. Y. Fung, which won the PEN USA Translation Award. His articles, stories, poems and translations have appeared internationally in more than 300 magazines and 40 anthologies.

JEROME SEATON is a Professor Emeritus of Chinese at the University of North Carolina, Chapel Hill. He is the translator of many books from the Chinese including *The Drifting Boat: Chinese Zen Poetry, Love and Time: Poems of Ou-Yang Hsiu*, *The Essential Chuang Tzu*, HYPERLINK "http://www.amazon.com/Dont-Bow-Buddhas-Selected-Poems/dp/1556591209/ref=sr_1_3?s=books&ie=UTF8&qid=1303938522&sr=1-3" *I Don't Bow to Buddhas: Selected Poems of Yuan Mei*, and *The Shambhala Anthology of Chinese Poetry*.

Bibliography

300 Tang Poems: A New Translation. Xu Yuanzhong, Loh Bei-yei and Wu Juntao, editors. Hong Kong: The Commercial Press, 1996.

Hawkes, David. *A Little Primer of Tu Fu.* Oxford: Oxford University Press, 1967.

Hucker, Charles O. *A Dictionary of Official Titles in Imperial China.* Stanford: Stanford University Press, 1985.

Indiana Companion to Traditional Chinese Literature. William H. Nienhauser, et al., eds. Bloomington: Indiana University Press, 1986 (volume 1) and 1998 (volume 2).

Qianshou tangren jueju 千首唐人绝句 (One Thousand Tang Quatrains). Fu Shou-sun 富寿荪, ed. Shanghai: Shanghai guji chubanshe, 1998.

Quan tang shi diangu cidian 全唐诗典故辞典 (Dictionary of Allusions in the Complete Tang Poems). Fan Zhilin 范之麟 and Wu Gengshun 吴庚舜, eds. Hubei cishu chubanshe, 1989. 2 vols.

Quan tang shi suoyin 全唐詩索引 (Index to the Complete Tang Poems). Shanghai: Shanghai guji chubanshe, 1990.

Quan tang shi 全唐詩 (The Complete Tang Poems). Shanghai: Shanghai guji chubanshe, 1985. 2 vols. Photo reprint of 1707 palace edition. [Note: complete text available in full-text searchable format at HYPERLINK "http://cls.admin.yzu.edu.tw/QTS/%5D" http://cls.admin.yzu.edu.tw/QTS/]

Tang caizi zhuan 唐才子傳 (Biographies of Tang Masters). Taipei: Taibei guji chubanshe, 1997. 2 vols.

Tangdai shiren liezhuan 唐代詩人列傳 (Biographies of Tang Poets). Feng Zuomin 馮作民, trans. Taibei: Xingguang chubanshe, 1982.

Tangdai wenxue shi 唐代文学史 (A History of Tang Literature). Qiao Xiang-zhong 乔象锺 and Chen Tiemin 陈铁民, chief editors. Beijing: Renmin daxue chubanshe, 1995. 2 vols.

Tangshi da cidian 唐诗大辞典 (The Great Dictionary of Tang Poetry). Zhou Xunchu 周勋初 chief editor. Nanjing: Jiangsu guji chubanshe, 1990.

Tangshi Sanbai Shou Xiangxi 唐詩三百首詳析 (Three Hundred Tang Poems, Analyzed in Detail). Yu Shouzhen 喻守真, editor and annotator. Hong Kong: Taiping shuju, 1965.

Tangshi Sanbai Shou Xinyi 唐詩三百首新譯 (Three Hundred Tang Poems, Newly Translated). Qiu Xieyou 邱燮友, annotator and translator. Taipei: Sanmin shuju, 1998.

Tangshi Sanbai Shou 唐詩三百 (Three Hundred Tang Poems). Ding Xuzhou 丁序周, translator. Taipei: Wuzhou Chubanshe, 1986. [Pirated bilingual edition with English translations from *Jade Mountain*.]

Tangshi Sanbai Shou 唐詩三百 (Three Hundred Tang Poems). Hong Kong: Guangzhi shuju, n.d.

Tangshi Sanbai Shou 唐詩三百首 (Three Hundred Tang Poems). Zhuang Huiyi 莊惠宜, annotator and translator. Taipei: Wenguo shuju, 1998.

Times Atlas of China. New York: The New York Times Book Company, 1974.

Tōdai no shijin 唐代の詩人 (Tang Poets). Hiraoka Takeo 平岡武夫 and Ichihara Kōkichi 市原亨吉, eds. Kyoto: Kyoto daigaku jimbun kagaku kenkyusho, 1960.

Xie zhu tangshi jueju 谢注唐诗绝句 (Xie's Notes on Tang Quatrains). Hangzhou: Zhejiang guji chubanshe, 1988. Annotation by Xie Fangde 谢枋得 (d.1288) of an earlier anthology by Zhao Fan 赵蕃 (d. 1229) and Han Hu 韩淲 (d. 1224).

Zhongguo dimingⅼü: Zhonghua renmin gongheguo dituji diming suoyin 中国地名录: 中华人民共和国地图集地名索引 (Gazetteer of China: An Index to the Atlas of the Peoples Republic of China). Beijing, Ditu chubanshe, 1983.

Zhongguo lishi dituji, sui tang wudai shiguo shiqi 中国历史地图集隋唐五代十国时期 (Historical Atlas of China: Sui, Tang, Five Dynasties and Ten Kingdoms Periods). Tan Qixiang 谭其骧, chief editor. Beijing: Ditu chubanshe, 1982.

Zhongguo nianli zongpu 中國年歷總譜 (Chronological Tables of Chinese History). Tung Tso-pin (Dong Zuobin), ed. Hong Kong; Hong Kong University Press, 1960. 2 vols.

Zhongguo wenxuejia da Cidian: Tang Wudai zhuan 中国文学家大辞典: 唐五代卷 (Encyclopedic Dictionary of Chinese Literati: Tang and Five Dynasties Volume). Beijing: Zhonghua Shuju, 1992.

Zhonghua renmin gonggheguo dituji 中华人民共和国地图集 (Atlas of the Peoples Republic of China). Beijing: Ditu chubanshe, 1984.

Zhongwen da cidian 中文大辭典 (The Encyclopedic Dictionary of the Chinese Language). Zhang Qiyun 張其昀, chief editor. Taipei: The Chinese Academy, 1962–68. First revised edition, 1973. 10 vols.

Acknowledgments (continued)

Spoon River Quarterly: "Seeing Meng Haoran Off to Yangzhou (Seeing Meng Haoran Off from Yellow Crane Tower)," "Poem Sent to Old Friends while Staying Overnight on the Tunglu River"

The Book Press: "Invitation to Liu Nineteen," "The Chancellor of Shu," "The Eight Formations," "Seeking a Hermit but Not Finding Him"

The Coe Review: "A Ballad of Lovely Women"

The MacGuffin: "The Ancient Cypress," "At the Grave of Grand Marshal Fang," "Elegies on Ancient Sites (5)"

The Literary Review: "Gazing at Mount Tai,"

The New Press Literary Quarterly: "A Woman of Quality"

Wordsmith: "Dreaming of Li Bai (1)."

Michael Farman's translations have appeared in the following journals, to whose editors he would like to express his gratitude:

Bellingham Review: "Cicada," "Untitled (Last night's stars, last nights winds)"

Passport: "Mount Zhongnan (A looming presence near the capital)"

The Literary Review: "Untitiled (In this disastrous year of famine)"

We would also like to thank the editors of the following publications in which some of Geoffrey Waters' translations first appeared:

EROTIC CHINESE POETRY: "In the Palace," "Sharing My Feelings," "Given in Parting (1)," "Given in Parting (2)"

Evansville Review: "The Song of Endless Sorrow"

Guernica: "To a Friend Lost in the Tibetan War"

Renditions: "Spring Sadness," "Sharing My Feelings," "Autumn Night"